ENDORSEME

"Steve Grant has lived through the unimaginable and yet has had the courage to turn his family pain from multiple losses from addiction into action. *Don't Forget Me* is a powerfully inspirational personal journey of Steve rising up against intense stigma to face the reality, and instigate the community transformation needed so that other families don't experience his reality."

Greg Williams
Award-Winning Filmmaker of The Anonymous People and
Generation Found

"The worst thing imaginable happened to Steve Grant. And then it happened again. Yet Steve, his message and this book are far less about the despair of bad things happening, and much more about the hope and possibility that remains. It's an amazing, tragic and redemptive story that needed to be shared and needs to be read."

John O'Leary
#1 National, Bestselling Author of *On Fire*

"When we as parents struggle with raising our children, it is easy to think that we are alone. Steve Grant's new book, *Don't Forget Me*, says otherwise. From his deep pain of losing both his sons to addiction, he has written their stories and become an advocate and encourager for other parents. He offers hope and priceless counsel from someone who has walked that difficult road. This is a must read."

Judge Michael A. Corriero (Ret.).
Author of *Judging Children as Children: A Proposal for a Juvenile Justice System*

"Thanks for your help, Steve. The Opiate Epidemic, specifically, as well as other expanding addiction problems, including those caused by alcohol and other drugs, are taking an immense toll on our economy while tearing apart our social fabric. Steve Grant generously shares one family's fight in this "war against drugs." Countless other American families have fought the good fight and lost! This is heartbreaking for the survivors. Now through Steve's efforts, readers can also share in his family's struggles and, perhaps, glean some information on what works and does not. As Steve concludes, hope lies in education and more research to engage the enemy at the root causes of addiction, which lie in brain mechanisms, in social and educational institution responses, accompanied by enlightened law enforcement and judicial processes. We should all applaud the efforts that Steve Grant expended to save his own family, but, even more so, we should be thankful for his courage and wisdom to share his experience. By doing so, hopefully others might find solace and be better equipped to deal with similar issues in their lives and families. Sadly for all of us, Steve Grant's story is not unique, but thankfully, sharing it is – and this has great value!"

Raymond F. Anton, MD
Thurmond Wellness Endowed Chair,
Distinguished University Professor
Professor of Psychiatry – Addictions Sciences Division
Scientific Director – Alcohol Research Center
Director of the Clinical Neurobiology Laboratory
Medical University of South Carolina

"When I first met Steve Grant he was searching for his life's mission and purpose. After reading *"Don't Forget Me"* I am certain he found it. This book and his work are sure to make a difference in many lives."

Ben Newman
Performance Coach and Keynote Speaker

"Steve Grant's book, *Don't Forget Me*, is a powerful story that will speak to so many families impacted by the nation's opioid crisis. The book offers a truthful look at how one family did the best they could to help two sons who struggled with addiction. Though both Steve's sons died due to this horrible disease, the fact he is willing to openly talk about the pain of his family's loss means that he has gained perspective that can and will help other families."

Wood Marchant, '89, LISW-CP
Director, Collegiate Recovery Program, College of Charleston,
Division of Student Affairs

Don't Forget Me

Don't forget me

A Lifeline of HOPE for Those Touched by Substance Abuse and Addiction

STEVE M. GRANT

NEW YORK

LONDON • NASHVILLE • MELBOURNE • VANCOUVER

Don't Forget Me

A Lifeline of HOPE for Those Touched by Substance Abuse and Addiction

Published in New York, New York, by Morgan James Publishing. Morgan James is a trademark of Morgan James, LLC. www.MorganJamesPublishing.com

ISBN 9781642795486 paperback
ISBN 9781642795493 eBook
Library of Congress Control Number: 2019938263

Cover Design by:
Megan Dillon
megan@creativeninjadesigns.com

Interior Design by:
Chris Treccani
www.3dogcreative.net

Morgan James is a proud partner of Habitat for Humanity Peninsula and Greater Williamsburg. Partners in building since 2006.

Get involved today! Visit
MorganJamesPublishing.com/giving-back

For all of the beautiful, amazing people who struggle with substance use disorders and to all of those who love them.

In loving memory of Dorothy Grant

TABLE OF CONTENTS

Acknowledgments   *xv*

Introduction   *xvii*

Disclaimer   *xix*

Chapter 1   **Beginnings**   **1**

                   Getting Started   1

                   Expecting   4

Chapter 2   **Christopher**   **7**

                   Our First Born   7

                   School Days and Friday Nights   18

                   I Don't Want to Be a F*** Up   20

                   Finding Help   22

                   Drug Tests and Following the Trail   25

                   Progression   31

                   Mailbox   34

                   You Want Me to Leave My House   35

                   Finding Help 2   36

                   Letters from Rehab   42

                   All I Do is a Little Weed   48

                   Aftercare and the Abbeville Experiment   49

	In Between	53
	It's Not Always as It Seems	58
	Cried Three Times	62
	The Worst 28 Days	63
	Houston, We Have Liftoff	67
	Déjà vu	68
	The Death of a Son	72
	Aftermath	74
	Patterns	79
Chapter 3	**Kelly**	**83**
	Mr. Big Shot	83
	The Teen Years	88
	A Change of Scenery	91
	Marching to His Own Beat	93
	Struggles	98
	Every Loss is Different	105
Chapter 4	**HOPE**	**107**
	Remembering	107
Chapter 5	**Some Things I Learned and Experienced Along the Way**	**111**
	Next	111
	We Need Each Other	114
	It is a Process, Not an Event	116
	Just Say Yes	118
	Control and Influence	120
	Ask Questions	122
	There is Honor in Grief	126
	There is Hope	127

Conclusion   **The Good That Follows**   **131**

    Gratitude and Testimonials   138

About the Authors   **141**

    Steve Grant   141

    James E. Campbell, LPC, LAC, MAC, CACII   142

Acknowledgments and Gratitude   **143**

    From Steve   143

    From James   144

Weed and the Adolescent Brain   **145**

Resources   **147**

ACKNOWLEDGMENTS

James Campbell has become a wonderful friend over the past several years. This book has been a dream of mine for many years, but I needed someone to help me articulate the stories of my sons. I specifically wanted to work with a clinician who understood "the why" and "the how" of the disease of addiction and how it affects the lives of your entire family.

I approached James in 2017, knowing his profession and that he has written two prior books, to help me tell my story. He graciously accepted, and I believe he has done a great job using his extensive experience and knowledge of adolescent and young adult addiction and applying it to my family's story.

The story in my heart was already powerful, but with James's help, the book became much more than simply sharing the details about Christopher and Kelly. Thank you, James, for helping me to find the words.

I would also like to thank Stacey Bevill. I am grateful for her editing skills and assistance in preparing this book for publication.

INTRODUCTION

In light of the recent opioid epidemic, there are countless articles, stories, television shows, and movies about addiction and the repercussions of it. This story is different. It is different because it is mine.

When addiction hits home, everything changes.

Statistics could not move me, but my sons could.

"Epidemics" did not scare me, but seeing my sons struggle with an illness would.

News stories lacked the power to compel me to action, but my children's story did.

When a life is touched by addiction, it is not about statistics. It is about people. In this case, those people are my sons Chris and Kelly.

This is not a story about statistics and epidemics. This is a story about being a parent, about loving someone struggling with substance use, and about loss. It is also a story about what comes after loss. What, if anything, rises from the ashes of grief? It is a story about recovery.

This is a story about hope and knowing that none of us ever has to walk alone.

DISCLAIMER

As I have written this story, I want to honor the truth that I can only tell from my point of view. I have done my very best to fact-check everything that is recorded in these pages and to share the story of my sons faithfully. That said, I acknowledge that each story is told from my perspective, and everything contained herein is told through the lens of how I see and remember them.

Any omissions, errors, and oversights are due to my imperfect memory. No ill will is intended to anyone in any regard.

There are five occasions in this book where profanity is referenced. I do not wish to be offensive or gratuitous in the use of expletives; I want to be true to the struggles and challenges that we faced and convey the truth of the lives we lived at the time.

Understanding that some of those who read this book may be in recovery from substance use disorders, I do want to acknowledge that there are some references to drug use that could be triggering for some. Although these descriptions are not overly graphic, they are honest, and I would not want any readers to be caught unaware.

Lastly, whenever possible, I have sought to honor the anonymity and confidentiality of others in this story. In that regard, I have attempted to not specifically reference individuals who are in recovery or actively using substances or any treatment centers by name.

BEGINNINGS

Getting Started

I was born in New York City and lived in the area until 18 years of age in Paramus, New Jersey. My twin brother, Anthony, and I are the oldest siblings; we have a younger brother, Freddy. I also had a younger sister named Robin. Growing up I was an exceptionally average student, but I found a bit of a niche for myself in athletics with both basketball and baseball.

My younger years were unexceptional for the most part. We walked to high school daily and stayed out of any major trouble. Following high school, I attended Furman University on a small baseball scholarship and graduated in 1980.

During my sophomore year of college, my younger sister died in a car accident at the age of eighteen. I recall riding with my family to identify her body near the Jersey shore and my mother crying throughout the round trip. After that things began to change within my family.

Growing up, we had alcohol in our basement. It was essentially the same bottles for years. After my sister's death, the bottles began to change. During that time my father manufactured mink coats in the garment district in New York City, which meant he left early and came home late. Mom began drinking while Dad was at work. This was not new for her family, just for her. My mom's mother drank alcohol daily and was seldom seen without a shot glass. My mom's brother died in his fifties from alcoholism. Her youngest brother was told by his doctor that if he drank again, he could die. That was over thirty years ago, and he hasn't had a drink since. My mom's drinking should not have come as a shock, considering the family's history. Fortunately, mom was able to quit drinking with some treatment and support. Our family tree was watered, in part, by alcohol.

I continued my education at Furman and was captain of the baseball team in both my junior and senior years. After I graduated from college, I worked for my father for six months in New York, and during that time, I married a young woman named Mary, whom I met at Furman. She was from Connecticut, about an hour away from where we lived, and we married in 1981. Mary and I moved to Greenville, SC in February of 1982 where I began working in the financial services business. From that perspective, the story sounds pretty linear, and as though everything worked out well. I wish that I could tell you that was the case.

Mary was from an upper-middle-class family and was one of six kids. She fell in the middle of the birth order. She was teased mercilessly at times growing up, which probably did not do a great deal to build her sense of self-worth. Once we were married, I attempted to stand up for her at times with her family, but my attempts fell on deaf ears.

Not only was Mary's family a little wealthier and teased more fiercely than mine, but they also had another identifying feature. The family drank more regularly than mine. They didn't drink to excess at that time; they typically had a few martinis after work. Faced with this I did what any self-respecting son-in-law would do—I began drinking martinis too.

Mary had a real knack for languages and spoke three. She was working outside of the home when we learned we were expecting our first child. On May 16, 1984, we had a beautiful baby boy, and we named him Christopher. After his birth, she was a full-time homemaker. I vividly recall a conversation we had in our driveway upon bringing Chris home. I told Mary that we had committed an unselfish act in having our son and that we had to make him the center of our family. From that point forward, I essentially put Mary after Chris. When our second son, Kelly, was born on May 12, 1986, Mary moved to third place in terms of my priorities. I vividly remember this conversation and this attitude because both of them were equally, phenomenally wrong.

Children are an amazing gift and they have a powerful impact on families. They do not fare well as the center of a household. Children need a secure base to grow on and launch from; they can't be that base for themselves or for their parents. In that regard, I was putting unreasonable expectations on Chris before he ever arrived. Secondly, placing a child ahead of a spouse is a recipe for disaster. When we do that, we are inviting a child to play one parent against the other. This is not because the child is bad; it is because that's part of being a child. By putting Mary in second place to our children, I placed a wedge between us without even knowing it. It was a mistake made in ignorance, but ignorance does not release us from experiencing the repercussions of our choices. It's an occupational hazard of being human.

There are no perfect parents, and Mary and I were no exception. We made sure the boys brushed their teeth every night. We signed report cards. We all went to church every week. The early years were relatively peaceful in our household. In retrospect, it was the calm before the storm, but it was a wonderful time of making memories together. The cracks were already there, but they had not yet begun to show. That would soon change.

Having a child is an unselfish act, and now we had the challenge and privilege of raising this child. The problem is that rather than my wife and I being the center of the wheel with our children rotating around a solid, secure center, our children became the hub.

Expecting

When a couple conceives and is preparing to have a child, one of the words used to describe the process is that the couple is "expecting." Truer words may have never been spoken. From the moment I became aware that we would be having a child, I began expecting. I expected Christopher would be athletic and would make the teams he tried out for with all that would entail. I expected he would be a good student, would be outgoing, would share my faith, and a world of other things. I was expecting every bit as much as Mary was! To have a child is to see one's hopes take on a physical form. That is a frightening thing for a parent-to-be, but it is also a tremendous burden for the little one who has not even arrived on the scene. They are about to be born into a world of expectations.

Some of the expectations that we hold for our children are met, and some are not. Frustration is the distance between the two. One of the hallmarks of a healthy parent is that we learn to love our children through the disappointment, to love them for who they are and not devalue them because of who we expected they would be. That is the kind of father I wanted to be, and it is the kind of father I have learned to become. I am getting a bit ahead of myself. Let me tell you about my sons.

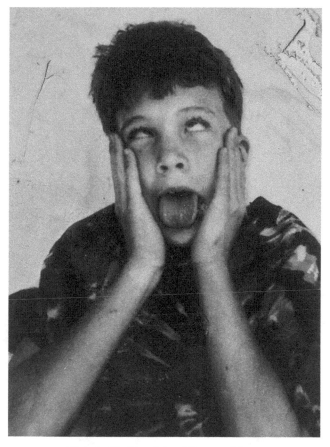

This is Chris at his silliest and best.
It captures his personality beautifully.

CHRISTOPHER

Our First Born

Christopher Roberts Grant was born on May 16, 1984. He was our first born, and I suppose in retrospect, we indulged him. He basically had a "normal" childhood, and Mary and I were blissfully oblivious as to the challenges of childhood and what that might entail. When Chris went to five-year-old kindergarten, we packed all of our hopes and dreams into the book bag with him the same way that most every parent does. Of course, it did not take long before we got our first glimpse that things may be a little different than we had anticipated. When we met Chris's 5-K teacher about his moving up to first grade in the fall, she suggested that he might benefit from repeating his current grade. She suggested that he was "a little wild" and even said that he was "a prime candidate for Ritalin." We knew he was energetic, but the rest came as a bit of a shock.

Being held back in kindergarten was not as common then as it is now, and it came with a healthy amount of stigma. We were not eager for him to start out with the deck stacked against him; but even so, we wanted to explore this with Chris. Mary and I agreed that I would take the lead in talking to him. I gave it a lot of thought and prepared what I believed was a fairly smooth response. I looked at my five-year-old son and said, "Christopher, your teacher loves you so much that she wants to teach you again next year."

Without missing a beat, Chris looked up at me with big trusting eyes and asked, "Will my friends still be in my class?" I paused a moment then replied that his teacher wanted *him* to stay with her.

Chris responded matter-of-factly, "Well then I don't want to do that then."

I was the man of the house. Mary and I were the parents, and Chris was the child. We responded accordingly by changing schools so that he wouldn't know that he was staying in the same grade.

To make it possible for Chris to be able to move to a new school, multiple things would have to happen, and those things seemed unlikely to fall into place. Nonetheless, I watched in amazement as everything worked out as though by divine intervention. Mary was asked to take on a teaching job at the other school, and she accepted the position on the condition that Chris would be able to come to the school with her. They agreed. Chris started there that fall and stayed at this school through the ninth grade. He made a lot of close friends there and began to spread his wings a bit as he grew. As a father, it was exciting to see!

Although Chris was often popular and seemed to have many friends, school was not without its challenges. Academics seem to come easy for some kids, but that wasn't always the case for Chris. It was not that Chris wasn't smart; he was extremely bright. Chris struggled to keep organized and often didn't remember to turn in his assignments even after he completed them. His level of ability wasn't the issue; most teachers chalked it up as a lack of effort or the need to focus. Teacher comments on report cards and evaluations during this time often included references to his not giving his best work and not paying attention in class. Nonetheless, he continued to do well enough to pass and move through his academic years and advanced year after year untilhe finally reached his teens.

While Chris was fourteen and in eighth grade, two things happened:

One was his confirmation into the church.

The other was that he began using alcohol and other drugs for the first time.

Chris's confirmation was met with incredible support both from family and friends. Chris's church basketball coach served as his sponsor for confirmation. He was important to Chris and consistently showed care and support for him. I have the confirmation letter that Mary and I wrote to him acknowledging his compassionate heart towards his great-maternal-grandmother. I have the letter that his maternal grandad wrote to him, sending him a picture of his own confirmation. In it, my father-in-law mentioned the first baseball game that he ever went to, a double-header between the Dodgers and Cardinals at Ebbets field. That connection to baseball ran deep through the family and made its way to Chris as well.

While Chris did not always shine in the classroom, he did shine in other areas. For one, Chris seemed to have a natural penchant for theater. He was cast in two different roles during his school years. One was as a DJ who ran a school in a popular play. Essentially for ninety minutes Chris got to dance and move to the music as the DJ. This was a stroke of genius on the part of the director; Chris had trouble standing still at the best of times. One of Chris's liabilities was turned it into an asset! He also starred in *Forrest Gump* as Forrest. In both roles, Chris seemed to have a natural talent and excelled. He also excelled in math.

Chris demonstrated natural talent on the athletic field. That was not entirely a surprise. After all, with my legacy of athleticism, I was sure he was destined for greatness! Chris, like me, had a natural bend towards athletics, but it took it some time to manifest itself. I had been the same way. My passion had been for baseball as a child as well, but early on I was the kid who volunteered to play on the other team when they didn't have enough players. It killed my parents that I had so much love for the game but could not hit a Volkswagen if it had been pitched to me before I was twelve. Then one day it was as though a light came on and I was able to hit. The same thing happened with Chris. He started slowly, but he got better quickly as he got older. I even coached his team from the time that he was young and was in many ways, one of his biggest cheerleaders!

Later Chris excelled in soccer. We spent Thanksgiving in Atlanta and Christmas in Orlando for tournaments. Either Mary or I went with him. We didn't go as a family because Kelly had no interest in it. We went the route that was easier for everybody, but the choice separated our family. We never did anything as a family. I did things with Chris and Mary did things with Kelly, but it was never the four of us.

Despite his natural inclination to athletics, sometimes his effort was not as strong as it could have been. Chris didn't always see how gifted he was athletically, and because of that he did not always apply himself as strongly as he could have. This is a trait I'm afraid he came by honestly, as I often heard the same thing both growing up and in my work life as I grew older as well.

The reality was that although Chris had a world of potential in him, he never seemed to feel at ease in his skin. It was as though he was acting in his own life at times instead of living it. He seemed to think that he had to be someone other than himself to be liked or loved by others.

When he looked in the mirror, he simply didn't see what I and others saw. This was not always clear, but I was about to get a crash course on how he saw himself.

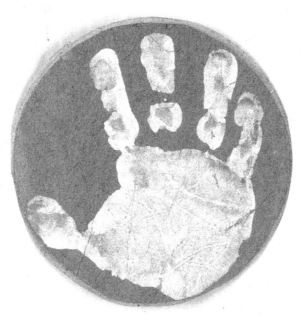

It's amazing my heart could fit in such a small hand!
This is Chris's handprint from school.

Chris was always a loving child. This is an ornament he made for me
when he was only four years old. The feeling was mutual!

Sometimes you get discouraged
Because I am so small
And always leave my fingerprints
On furniture and walls.

But every day I'm growing—
I'll be grown up someday
And all those tiny handprints
Will surely fade away.

So here's a final handprint
Just so you can recall
Exactly how my fingers looked
When I was very small.

Christopher Grant
1987

Another project that I held on to through the years is this poem with Chris's hands from when he was three years old.

May '89

Christopher is a delight to have in class. He comes in with a smile and wonderful attitude every day. Though he has come a long way this year, I still believe it would be best to give him more time to develop in these areas:

1) fine motor control
2) attention span
3) following directions

Because he is young and a boy, these things

Note from 5K teacher

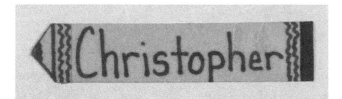

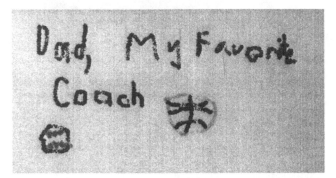

I love that I got the opportunity to coach both of my sons. This is a card that Chris made for me when he was still small. They were my favorite players as well, and I was glad to be leading their team!

CRG
12/92

```
2›        I got a Compuiter,basebball bat
,baseball,football,Word Munchers,
Golf club set,Monopulee game,
Sonic 2 Sega Genesis game.
  ON Christmas Day I went to my
Grannys house.On Christmas
vacatition I went to see to movies
 Home Alone2  and Mighty Ducks .
```

In many ways, Chris was a very normal child. At eight-years-old, he wrote about sports, board games, family, and movies. Many people think that a "certain kind" of person grows up to become addicted. Although it's scary, the truth is that anyone can develop a substance use disorder. Addiction does not discriminate.

504 ACCOMMODATION PLAN
for
Christopher Grant

Mr. and Mrs. Stephen Grant, parents of Chris (DOB 5/16/84), presented
████████ High School with a request that classroom accommodations be made
for Chris in accordance with Section 504 of the Rehabilitation Act of 1973:
Handicapped Persons Rights under Federal Law. ████████████, MD, of
████████ Psychiatry, PA, has diagnosed Chris as having ADHD. Chris is being
treated medically for this disability.

The following are reasonable classroom accommodations that were agreed
upon:

1. Up to 50% additional time should be allowed for tests. Chris will let
    the teacher know if he needs this additional time. Arrangements for
    him to complete testing with additional time will be made between
    Chris and the teacher, based on mutual convenience.

2. Chris should be seated near the center of instruction.

Copy: Parents
       Teachers
       Student Cumulative Folder
       504 Accommodations Book

*Chris's struggle to "keep organized" was not without good reason. He was
later diagnosed and treated for ADHD. Chris had what was called a 504
Plan to give him accommodations related to his diagnosis. Often those
with ADHD are never diagnosed. Chris was able to get help and support,
but school was not a place where he felt successful. This may have been
part of his not feeling comfortable in his own skin.*

Dear Christopher,

I hear you're preparing for Confirmation. I'm sure your teachers will tell you that's the sacrament in which the Holy Spirit gives you the strength necessary to live a good Christian life. In my day we were told that Confirmation makes you a soldier for Christ – today I think it's more " becoming a mature Christian." Same thing.

I went to an old photo album and found this picture of me on the big day. Notice I didn't have black shoes with my dark suit. The nuns didn't care for that, but they let me go ahead. After the ceremony my father took me and a friend to Ebbets Field to see a Dodgers-Cardinals double-header – my first major league game!

Anyway, study hard. I'm sure I'll see you before too long. I may need some help with my new computer, now that I've mastered word-processing.

Love,

Grandad

Our family was proud of Chris's love for the church and his confirmation.

This is the photo that was enclosed with the letter from Chris's maternal grandad on his confirmation day.

School Days and Friday Nights

Although we did not know it at the time, Chris often felt awkward in social situations. As I mentioned before, he didn't seem to feel at home in his own skin and struggled socially at times even though he was generally well-liked and popular.

One day a customer said to me, "I understand your son is a drunk, great athlete, but he's a drunk." He wouldn't tell me who told him about Chris's drinking, but I thought, hmm, that's an interesting comment...maybe something was going on. I would have loved to have known how the person that told me my son was a drunk knew. If he wasn't going to reveal the source, why did he make the statement? If I had known who it had come from, I might have believed it. It is incredibly difficult to get to the point where you're ready to face the seriousness of the situation. I thought he was being a teenager, doing what boys do.

Chris medicated his feelings of anxiety. We later learned that as early as eighth grade, Chris had begun drinking alcohol before Friday night football games. We were oblivious at first, but we were starting to follow a path of breadcrumbs towards the truth.

Of course, some of these breadcrumbs were more obvious than others. One of the first appeared when we were having the carpets cleaned at the house. After they finished, one of the workers mentioned that there were a lot of beer cans under our couch.

Beer cans? Under the couch at our house? Apparently, they were magic beer cans, because not a soul in our home had any idea how they had gotten there. That made no sense to me at the time, but it was one of the first steps down the trail.

It was around this time that Mary and I would go out of town on occasion and entrust the house to our sons for the evening. We had the sense that there were people over, and parties being hosted by them in our absence. We made it abundantly clear there was to be no one over while we were gone.

When Mary and I came home after our next trip, I was frankly, pleasantly surprised that the house seemed to be in order. I even checked the garbage can and under the furniture and saw no evidence that concerned me. Sometimes a father has a bit of a sixth sense and leaving well enough alone had never been my strength.

There was a tall fence at the back of our property, slightly taller than me. I decided to go and have a look at the other side. I got the ladder and went to the back of the yard, climbed up, and looked over. I was slack-jawed! On the other side of the fence, there were trash bags full of beer cans and stacks of empty pizza boxes. I decided to have a word with my son.

Chris, of course, denied having any idea how the cans and boxes got there. He responded with a perfectly reasonable sounding, "I couldn't eat that much pizza!" I pointed out that he couldn't alone but that he possibly could with help from his friends. Still, he denied it. Denial in the face of the obvious was to become a recurring theme in our household.

It occurred to me that there might be a way to get some additional clarity about this particular situation. I retrieved one of the boxes and took it to the pizza company where it was purchased. I had coached the owner's son in baseball, and we had remained friends. I explained that some boxes had been dropped on my property and asked if they could scan the bar code and let me know who had purchased the pizza. They scanned the box and then proceeded to give my son's name, our address, and the amount he had paid for the order. Even though the breadcrumbs were obvious, Chris initially denied that they were his or that he knew anything about them.

Other crumbs were more subtle.

I began to notice white spots–flecks really on the kitchen floor. These spots were small, and they were extremely difficult to get up. I tried to figure out where they were coming from, but I couldn't put a finger on it. Later I finally realized that it was from a bottle of scotch. When drops would fall on the floor and dry, they left behind the hard, white spots. Chris had inadvertently been dripping alcohol on the floor when he and his friends were drinking, and these little spots were like small crumbs of evidence.

Although I in no way condoned this, I knew that teens sometimes experimented. The trail was concerning, but I still didn't realize the gravity of the problem. That was about to change.

I Don't Want to Be a F*** Up

As I mentioned, Chris was confirmed into the church and his faith at fourteen as well. Chris was not perfect, but he was a good kid. He went to church with us regularly. He pulled passing grades academically. Chris was doing great in sports and was the only freshman on the varsity basketball and soccer teams. By all accounts, he was doing well! That is why what happened next was such a shock.

One evening in 1999, I was reading in the den of our home like I often did. Chris came down in his pajamas and said he wanted to talk to me. He sat next to me, and we had a deep father and son conversation. He said, "I don't want to be a f*** up, Dad."

I remember sitting there and wondering what does he mean? I knew that there was more to this conversation then he was able to communicate. He was 6'0" and was 170 lbs. He was a beautiful boy, was exceling in sports and was popular in school. He had all kinds of girls, all sorts of friends. And he was a freshman on his high school teams. By all accounts, that was the last thing he should be saying to me.

I asked him what would lead him to think that he was in any way a f*** up.

He could not articulate what he meant that night; and, though I kept asking, I could not decipher what he was trying to tell me. I knew on some level that he was trying to convey something important to me, but I had no idea what exactly that might be. I thought about that moment several times over the next few days, mulling it over and trying to piece together what he might be thinking to no avail. It was a puzzle that gnawed at my mind as the days passed.

A couple of nights later, he came back to me and said, "You're my only friend in this world."

Now that got my attention, and I knew that something was wrong. I had helped to start the suicide prevention hotline in Greenville, SC, and had gone through some training to understand how to have a phone conversation with someone who was struggling. Through this, I knew some of the words and phrases that were cause for concern.

Typically, someone that's going to kill themselves will put out signs and say things in a subtle way. They might not say, "I'm going to kill myself." They are more likely to say things like, "You're my best friend in this world," or "I'm sorry if I ever caused you any problems," or "I'm so thankful that we were friends." These are statements that can be considered ultimate and finishing.

Although this did not technically point towards any suicidal ideation for Chris, it had a discordant ring to it that shook me. The gnawing grew louder at that moment.

Chris and I had a pretty good relationship, but I remembered being 15 and was sure that by that time, my father had dropped a few rungs as far as being my best friend. I realized that he was trying to tell me something, but I had no idea what.

In retrospect, he was telling me he was using, that it was getting worse, and that he didn't know what to do, but at the time he didn't have the words. I knew that we were going to need some help to figure things out.

Finding Help

I was not entirely certain where to start; the next morning, I jumped to the phones and reached out to a local pediatrician for some guidance. After explaining my concerns to him about Chris, the pediatrician suggested a child psychiatrist in our area, but he was quick to add that he was not certain whether he was taking new patients. My friend went on to ask when I might want to see the psychiatrist, and I told him as soon as possible. When he saw how passionate I was about getting Chris some help, he advocated for me, and the psychiatrist agreed to meet with me during his lunch hour the next day. After meeting with me and hearing my concerns, he met Chris for an assessment. Afterward, he tried to explain what Chris was going through. He diagnosed Chris with Bipolar Disorder Not Otherwise Specified, Attention Deficit Disorder, Cannabis Abuse, and Alcohol Abuse Rule Out Dependence. He suspected that Chris's life was beginning to be controlled by marijuana and alcohol.

I was dumbfounded.

Once his addiction was confirmed by a professional, I knew I wouldn't be able to pray or hope it away.

Chris was prescribed medications to help him with his diagnoses. He was taking Paxil, Adderall, Depakote, and Wellbutrin to help him regulate his emotions and improve his focus. The psychiatrist noted that Chris tended to attribute his problems to others. Medications alone, although often critical to addressing mental health needs, are never enough in and of themselves to help those they are designed to serve. With that in mind, Chris's psychiatrist referred him to supportive counseling in April of 2000.

The therapist had told me, "You must take your family back, Steve." Chris met with his new therapist for four sessions in total. During the fourth session in June, we were sitting in the therapist's office, and I explained to Chris that we were going to take control of our house back and that he was going to start living by our rules again. These rules included taking his car keys if he couldn't produce a negative drug screen. It also included meetings for Chris with a therapist. The mistake I made was having Chris meet us there instead of us taking him with us. Chris refused to give up his keys. He was angry and left the session, went outside, got in his car, and drove off in the rain. The therapist told us not to worry and to stay where we were seated. Mary and I stayed to talk with the counselor to discuss what to do next, but before the end of the session, we got a call from Chris. He was in an accident.

It had rained most of the day, and the roads were wet. Chris was driving a Chevrolet Saturn that had been owned by my parents. He was driving too fast and was headed downtown soon before rush hour on a Friday. Chris was not a great driver. For as gifted an athlete as he was, he had terrible manual dexterity. He lost control of the vehicle, went through the median, across multiple lanes of oncoming traffic, and up an embankment on the opposite side of the road. His car flipped over and ended up on its roof. It was amazing that nobody was killed—him or anyone else. When we arrived at the scene of the accident, we were surprised to see his high school basketball coach was there. He had seen the accident and pulled over when he saw it was Chris. A policeman was also there, and I was worried Chris had been drinking. I was sure he was on something.

I was equal parts terrified and relieved. I put my arms around Chris, and told him, "It's on you. You know that you've just dodged a bullet. The Lord was watching over you." As I held my arms around my son, he began to cry. Maybe it was partly adrenaline or perhaps general morose, but this was one of only three times I saw Chris cry.

How many times can someone drive through heavy traffic and then flip their car a few times? I thought for sure the experience would make him sober. It was a humbling experience, but that didn't last for long. The accident happened because he was angry about the fact that we were attempting to draw a line in the sand and instill rules. It was scary. The young policeman didn't even give him a ticket or a warning, possibly because his coach and Mary and I were there providing support. I certainly didn't need one more legal issue. They towed the car away, and that was it.

I pass the site of the accident on my way to and from work. Each time I remember. I believe that God spared him that day for a reason.

Chris refused to return for sessions after that day, but Mary and I continued to meet for counseling through September of that year. One of the main things that became clear through our counseling is how differently we parented. I tended to be more of the nurturer in the relationship, and Mary often saw me as too lenient. On the other hand, she was more structured, and I tended to see her as too strict and rigid. The tension from Chris's struggle was applying pressure to our marriage, and the pressure was causing the cracks in the relationship to show. We were beginning to understand just how much trouble Chris was in…we all were in.

Eventually, we started family therapy. All four of us attended, which bothered Kelly. He did not want to be a part of it. There was an overriding concern for my well-being. My health was not good and was getting worse. The therapist went around the room and asked everyone who they were worried about the most. It wasn't Chris; they were concerned about me. I was only worried about Chris.

I remembered that I loved growing roses and doing yard work. I had stopped doing the activities that I enjoyed. It reminded me of seeing the "10 Signs of Depression" poster in the lobby of a doctor's office and counting off. Oh Lord, this is one, there's two, there's three, there's four, there's five, etc. I no longer had an interest in engaging in the hobbies I loved. I was depressed. I was so focused on Chris that

I hadn't noticed what was happening to me. Those sessions would ultimately break into an argument between Chris and his mother.

I saw a family practice doctor on a Saturday. He knew some of the struggles I was having. He shared the biblical analogy of crossing the river. I needed to be physically able to get to the other side. I was the person that everyone was counting on. My family needed me. I wasn't going to be there for them if I had a heart attack or a stroke. At one point, my blood pressure was about 180 over 140 instead of 110 over 70. The doctor sat me down and said, "This is what's going to happen here. You're the person that's needed the most in this whole process to save the ship. Right? You must be around to save the ship."

Drug Tests and Following the Trail

In light of the mounting evidence, I suspected Chris might be doing more than experimenting with alcohol. I decided to give him a drug test. I knew a lot of paramedical professionals who worked in the health field; I called and asked three of them to come over to drug test Chris. Why three? Because I had no idea how he would respond. Chris came home that afternoon through the back door. He was always polite, and he introduced himself to them. I told him we were going to drug test his urine. He handled it surprisingly well; he said he needed to go upstairs to put his bag down first. He went up and came right back down. Chris went in the bathroom off of the kitchen by himself to give the specimen. When he brought the cup out, he was told that the specimen he provided was not testable and couldn't be his urine. It was too cold and did not fall into the required temperature range.

I was confused because it was clear that it was urine in the cup. When I pressed Chris, he told me he had ordered urine off of the internet. It is important to note here that the internet wasn't what it is now, and buying things online was a relatively new concept.

The idea that someone could purchase urine from the internet was one of the most bizarre things I had heard at that point. Nonetheless, Chris showed me the receipt from his purchase. He used his own urine and tested positive for marijuana. At this point, I realized that Chris was far more deeply into his use than I could have imagined. Buying urine off the internet to help pass a drug test that he did not even know was coming was beyond anything I had ever encountered. It was around this time that Chris began wearing his hair extremely short. We thought it was for sports, but in retrospect, it was likely a misguided attempt to avoid a hair strand drug test. Looking back on this, it was like the drug addict's playbook or the playbook for parents, whichever side you were on of what would happen next. Somebody he knew had warned him that his dad and mom were eventually going to give him a drug test. It was probably the person that was selling him the drugs he was selling to other people.

As I mentioned, I've never been one to leave well enough alone. I took the receipt and called the person who had sold the urine to Chris. Once I explained who I was, the seller was quick to point out that he did not know what the urine would be used for. Really?! I pointed out how disingenuous that was. He then went on to explain to me that he had not broken any laws in providing it, which was, unfortunately, absolutely true.

Lacking legal backing, I attempted to appeal to his humanity. I asked, "Do you think that is a good business to be in?" His response was telling. He replied, "It's a tremendous business."

All of these breadcrumbs along the way seemed to be leading to a destination that I had never hoped to go, and I had no idea what might be ahead.

Throughout all of this, Chris continued to play sports and performed well athletically. One morning after he had played a great game the night before, Chris complained of not feeling well when he woke up. He said he thought he had pulled something in his leg and asked to go get it checked. I took him to a local physician, and Chris went in and met with the doctor. Once he was finished and came out, we went back out to the car. Chris began complaining that the doctor had only given him "Mobic" for pain. I remember thinking, he's a pharmacist now? What I didn't know then is that Mobic was a relatively weak painkiller. Apparently, Chris already knew that. He had hoped for something stronger like OxyContin or Hydrocodone to help with his "injury." Later it became apparent that the physician, a long-time friend and client, knew what Chris was doing and was subtly sending a message. Many people along the way knew what I didn't know or what I at least suspected. I might have listened, but maybe I wouldn't have believed them.

I didn't know then that Chris had a routine. He would put on his backpack and walk, or sometimes even run depending on how much time he had, from our home to the liquor store. The owner of the store would sell alcohol to Chris and his friends. Chris had a fake ID and would often buy for his friends as well. He would then hide it somewhere in the house and drink with his friends when they came over. Once I began to suspect this, I knew I had to do something about it. I decided to start by doing some investigating.

During this time, we had someone hired to help us keep the house clean. I decided to be direct and asked her if Chris was ever home during the day when we were at work. Her nonchalant response shocked me.

"All the time with friends."

He was supposed to be in school during that time. Fear began to set into the pit of my stomach. Emboldened by her answer, I decided to check with one more person who might be able to shed some additional light on things—our neighbor from directly across the street. This neighbor and his wife were an older couple. They paid attention to things, including what was going on at my house when I wasn't there. When I asked him if anyone came over while we were at work, he said that cars went in and out of our driveway all the time. He also said that people frequently dropped things into and got stuff out of the mailbox. Although it was early, in light of my neighbor's observations, I decided to take a long lunch and went into the house to wait and see what happened.

Sure enough, at lunchtime Chris came into the house with a friend. He quickly downplayed the entire situation, introducing him as a baseball player, probably so that I would think more of him. I told them that they should both get back to school and that they shouldn't come home for lunch anymore. They went upstairs for a few minutes before coming back downstairs and leaving. After they left, I went upstairs and found a bottle of vodka behind the sofa where they had been sitting.

From this point, things continued to progress in terms of Chris's drinking, drug use, and behavior. I began to find empty beer cans and large liquor bottles in the house and specifically in Chris's bedroom. He continued to use a fake ID to purchase alcohol. At one point he bought a half-gallon of vodka and was preparing to drink it with his friends. I caught him, took the alcohol, and discussed this with him. I explained a little bit about our family history with drinking and told him that he was starting out on third base with drinking because of it. Soon after, Chris responded by drinking an entire bottle of Dewar's Scotch that belonged to me. He replaced what he drank with water. When I confronted him, he said that some girls had come over and drank it. During a trip with me to Atlanta, I found beer cans under the bed in the hotel room where Chris slept. This time around, Chris didn't deny they were his. I also found a bottle of bourbon and a bag of marijuana in his friend's bag.

Chris failed two drugs tests for marijuana that same summer. The first time he used the urine he bought off the internet by tying the container to his leg to pass it off as his specimen. I later found a bottle with someone else's urine in his room. Throughout the summer, I continued to find more empty beer cans around the house. They were not hidden well, almost as if he wanted to get caught. When I confronted him, Chris's responses began to change slightly. Although he usually denied any involvement, now he would become irate and scream or shout. His temperament and disposition were horrible. He threatened his mom and grandparents using abusive language. He "ran away" a few times, usually coming back late at night. He stayed out one whole night. We thought we had lost him that night, but it would be several more years before he died. Finally, his friend's mother called to tell us that he was at her home, which made us feel a whole lot better. He refused to tell me his whereabouts when I confronted him. During the summer he not only totaled the previously mentioned car after leaving a therapy session, he also caused another accident by hitting a Camaro owned by a retired marine with my vehicle. This accident resulted in $6,000 worth of repairs. Whether he had been drinking or using on that occasion is unclear. During that same summer, Chris visited a friend. The friend's father found marijuana on Chris and called to tell me to come get him. Chris didn't deny it was his and said he bought it with his paycheck from his summer job. Chris promised me that night he wouldn't smoke again, but he admitted that he really liked smoking marijuana.

That summer, I found marijuana pipes and rolling papers in his pockets on several occasions. He smoked cigarettes daily. He said he was trying to quit but was having a hard time.

We started dreading Friday nights. This was the night he would drink the most. To feel worthy, he thought he had to be a little hammered before social interactions. Later I learned what Chris was drinking. He'd ask if I ever had vodka, another time if I'd ever had Southern Comfort, and then if I had ever had scotch. Later I learned that this was his way of telling me what he was drinking.

The following school year, Chris was caught with alcohol on three consecutive Fridays. On the first occasion, he was caught at a friend's house pouring a glass of Southern Comfort. He reported that he had brought it to the friend's house and had planned on drinking it before going to the football game at his old high school. He attempted to rationalize why he was drinking, but it was a pitiful attempt. He had promised me only an hour before he was caught that he would not drink. On the second Friday, Chris was again getting ready to go to a football game. Right before he left, he went in the bathroom and drank a half-pint of Southern Comfort and hid the bottle behind the dresser in his room. Again, only an hour before I had discussed with him that he could not drink and that what happened the prior Friday "better not happen again." I found the bottle in his room later that night. On the third Friday, Chris came in with a friend I had not met before at 2 pm and went upstairs to the den to use the internet. I thought I smelled liquor but wasn't sure. Later I found a large bottle of Southern Comfort wrapped in a t-shirt behind the sofa. When I confronted Chris, he denied it was his and said it must have been there from a long time ago.

Later that weekend, Chris came to me and said he had thrown away an unopened 24 pack of tall beers. I checked the garbage can. He did throw some beers away, but only three hadn't been opened.

Progression

Addiction is considered a progressive disease. What that means is, not only does the amount of drug used and frequency it is used go up, but likewise the behaviors and other problems related to the drug use progress as well. I saw this play out in a number of ways during this time. It got to the point where there was an expectation that there would be trouble.

We were trying to determine who his friends were and if they were into drugs. When I realized what was going on with my son, I called parents or close friends to warn them that they may not want their child hanging around Chris. I didn't know if the bad influence was Chris or his friends.

I told one friend and his wife, "You don't want your son hanging around with my son. I think Chris's into some crap, and I don't know who's doing what, but you don't want that for your son." This would get back to Chris when friends would say that they couldn't see him anymore and explain that I had talked to their parents. I still have parents thank me for warning them. When kids get involved with drugs, they often lose old friends and get new friends that are not good influences.

One night I was lying awake on the couch in the dark when Chris came down the hall. He crept up quietly, closer and closer to me. He leaned down with his face only a few inches above mine. I lay silently to see what he was doing. He was seeing if I was awake. He ultimately decided I was asleep and slipped out of the house. I waited quietly to see what he would do. From the window, I saw him leave the house and get into his friend's car that was parked just down the road. This was relatively early in the days of cell phones, but I called Chris and told him he needed to get back home. Thankfully, he did.

The incident above helped me to realize Chris had been being picked up by one of his friends in the neighborhood late in the evening after we were all asleep. Chris would make sure I was sleeping, and then he would leave when his friend pulled up in his dad's BMW 7 Series. Of course, one small problem with this was that both Chris and his friend didn't have a license to drive. They would take turns driving around the neighborhood. When they needed gas, they would stop and siphon someone's tank. This went on for a while until one night one of them ran into a fancy all-brick mailbox in front of someone's house. Fortunately for Chris, his friend's dad learned of it and did damage control. The next day the mailbox was like new, and no one else knew what had happened.

By this time, Mary was not comfortable with Chris remaining behind while I traveled. He had little respect for her and showed her no courtesy. I had to take Chris whenever I went out-of-town, and he always had to bring a friend along with him, it could never be just the two of us. Later, even when we would visit him in rehab for family days, he would ask us to bring a friend.

One trip we went to a Furman/Appalachian State football game in Boone, North Carolina, and stayed at a local hotel. On the way, I made it clear that the place we were going would not tolerate underage drinking. It was a dry county and since it was in another state that meant that we would have out of state tags. I warned them that kids from the university go to Blowing Rock to drink and play pool. I told them that if they were going to go around the campus of Appalachian State, they better have a license. I knew they had fake IDs and wanted them to know that they would get into trouble if they tried to pass a fake id in this town. I would hide my keys on these trips, but Chris would always find them.

I got to the point where I didn't sleep because of worry. This lack of sleep had been going on for many years. I stayed up with the boys as long as I could, but eventually I fell asleep.

Chris and his friend slipped out and took the car. I got the call that Chris was in jail after being charged with a DUI.

Not too long after that Chris was with me again during a business trip to Charleston, SC. Chris didn't bring a guest, instead he met a friend (the son of a prominent minister in the area) from the boarding school in Arden. Chris was there when I woke up, and I thought we had survived the trip unscathed. I was wrong. I started picking up on little things. I found out about the incident after I looked out the window the next morning and saw the car had been backed in. I always pull forward into a space.

Knowing that he had gone out the night before I said, "Christopher, all right, come clean on this whole deal. What's going on?" And he did, he was honest. I later found out that Chris and his friend took my car and went out drinking again. Chris was driving, but when they were pulled over by the police, he pushed his friend into the driver's seat saying that he couldn't get another DUI and that he wasn't even supposed to be driving. Chris's friend was charged, but I knew the truth of what happened. I apologized up and down to his parents the next day. Chris's friend was not permitted to hang out with him again.

I mentioned that Chris always had to have a friend with him. I would take my parents on vacations with us to the beach. One year my parents said they weren't going to go because Chris was once again bringing a friend. Chris overheard the conversation and felt insulted. He convinced my parents that they should come and reluctantly they joined us. My parents said that something always happens. And something did happen. Again.

We went to Isle of Palms. They agreed to come because it was a three-story house. Chris, a friend from boarding school, and Kelly stayed in the basement. Everyone could come and go as they pleased. The boys went out and dragged Kelly with them. I think Kelly went along many times even when he would have preferred not to go. They met a girl and she began drinking with them. I didn't know what had happened that night until a lady came and knocked on the door. She had her attractive young daughter who was about 12 or 13 years old with her. She was furious because her daughter had come home drunk and implicated Chris. She told me that her daughter had gotten in trouble for drinking because of him and that I should teach my son better.

My parents went home after that incident. They told me that even though I was paying for everything, it just wasn't relaxing. Chris took that hard. I understood how my parents felt and it hurt me. I leaned on them for emotional support. That was our last family vacation with my sons and my parents.

All of these stories are just the tip of the iceberg. For every story I have shared in these pages, there are five I haven't told. To love someone who is using drugs is hard. Trust gets eroded and fear creeps into the crevices of the relationship. You watch their light get a little bit dimmer than it was the day before, but you remember them in their full radiance. I was watching my son systematically make decisions that moved him progressively away from me and those who loved him most, and I was hurt and scared.

By all accounts, my son's drug use and the problems related to it were progressing quickly, and I was watching him spiral out of control right in front of me. As a result, even seemingly benign occurrences began to become suspect.

Mailbox

To some it may seem odd, but I connected with my sons daily and usually around the same time each day. I would call to touch base and see how their day had gone. During this time, it was common for Chris to call me to ask when I was coming home. When I told him what time I would be home, he would often ask if I would mind swinging by one of his friends' homes and picking up a CD for him from their mailbox. Since Chris was into music, I didn't think much of it at the time. It was not far out of the way, and the CD was always there. I didn't learn until much later why he called and asked me to do that. Chris was stalling me. He would ask me to pick up a CD to give a "friend" a chance to swing by and pick up or drop off drugs at our house. By the time I arrived back at home, they would already have left.

The music, like so many things for Chris, had become a servant of his addiction, a means to an end.

Unbeknownst to me, Chris was selling drugs in addition to using by this point. Between the alcohol, drugs, sneaky behaviors, and escalating use, things were coming to a head, and I was afraid for my son. I was afraid for my whole family.

Uncertain of what to do at the time, we did the best we could. I usually went to work like I always had. One day there was a wrinkle in the schedule.

You Want Me to Leave My House

I decided to come home a little early for lunch.

When I walked in Chris looked like a deer caught in headlights. He asked, "Dad! What are you doing here?"

I was not able to keep the pitch of my voice from trailing upward. "What are *you* doing here?"

Chris quickly began to explain. "Dad, you need to leave."

"What?"

"You need to leave."

I was dumbfounded. "You want *me*…to leave *my* house?"

"Dad, you don't want to be here right now. Some stuff is about to go down."

This was absurd! I didn't leave. I went upstairs instead to collect my thoughts for a moment. Shortly after going upstairs I heard noise outside and looked out of the window. Chris was in the middle of the street fighting with another boy. Traffic was backed up in both directions as they fought. I went downstairs as quickly as I could to try to intervene, but by the time I arrived, both boys had realized that neither of them was going to win this fight.

They quit fighting when they were both bleeding from the blows. Chris walked past me towards the house; looked up at the sky and spat out the words, "I hate this f***ing life."

All I could say was, "It doesn't have to be this way, Christopher."

I later learned that his fight was because either he owed someone money, or they owed money to him. Chris was continuing to sell drugs out of our home and was using part of what he was supposed to be selling. Issues around drug money showed up in many ways. In addition to the fight, our cars were damaged, and the house was toilet papered frequently. Incidents were escalating to the point that I was becoming fearful for my family. I was concerned about what might happen, not just to Chris, but to any of us.

I know there are probably more dark stories about the drinking, drugs, and dealing. Our house was near a bad neighborhood and Chris spent a lot of time over there. A guy from that area came to paint my house one day and tried to warn me that my son was over there and hanging out with the wrong people. I remember thinking, okay, well that's interesting. There were a lot of people trying to send me messages; I didn't want to hear them. It was just too hard to pull together.

Finding Help 2

Although I told Chris that "it didn't have to be" that way regarding his life, this event showed me clearly that it was that way.

From that day forward, I was on a mission to research rehab facilities and to do everything in my power to find help for my son.

It was around this time that Mary and I attended a faith-based parenting class together. I remember a number of things about this event, but the one thing that stands out most clearly from that class was the statement that a child was to be "a welcome addition to an already existing family." As I heard those words, I realized that was part of the problem. I had never viewed my household that way. I had put Chris and Kelly ahead of Mary since birth, and I had to admit to myself that it was not going well. The problem was that by now Chris was fifteen and Kelly was thirteen. They had a great deal of practice at being put first ahead of Mary, and they were not eager to relinquish that status. It wasn't their place to help me put Mary first; it was mine. I wish we had gone to that class when the kids were one and three like most of the parents in the class, but we hadn't. If there was going to be a change, it needed to come from me.

Sometimes we'd be lying in bed at night and hear Chris inside the house moving around. It was usually about one o'clock in the morning. Mary would express concern and I would reply, "Mary, what's going to happen here?" I preferred to hear him inside our home over wondering where he was, and if he was safe. I knew he was going to go to rehab; we had to play that hand. It comes to a point where you wonder, how do I get him there? How do I do this? Do I get an interventionist? What do I do?

It quickly became apparent that though I had begun looking for treatment centers, I was completely lost. I asked the psychiatrist who had initially met with Chris for recommendations, and he agreed that Chris needed residential treatment and provided me with a list of several suggested providers. At that time the only real option in the state had a waitlist of over two months. I didn't have two months. In addition, I learned that my insurance required that the facility be a part of a hospital system. This meant that I had to look out of state to find the help we needed.

After a lot of looking and reading, I came across a ninety-day program in Tennessee. I reached out to them and started the process to get Chris into the program. Once my mind was made up, I was not a wishy-washy parent. I was convinced that he had a real problem.

During this time, Mary and I would lie in bed and pray for Chris nightly. The sad truth is that although I believe in the power of prayer, prayers alone were not going to change his disease. We pray for someone who has cancer, but the person with cancer still needs to go to the doctor.

One night, in the midst of our praying, something disconcerting happened. Once again, Chris was downstairs in the middle of the night.

Mary screamed at me. To some people this may not seem like a big deal, but Mary never yelled. Ever. When she screamed in the bed that night, it was as though something in me snapped. I had a moment of clarity and got up and went downstairs to find Chris. Although it took this unusual, out of character shriek from Mary to move me, it turned out to be a good thing.

Chris and I talked for what felt like most of the night. He shared that he wanted to be dead. He was pitiful. He said, "All I really wanted to be Dad, is like you and Uncle Anthony, helping people and serving people." I thought, oh my God, this kid has been conditioned to believe that he's helping his friends by selling them marijuana or getting them liquor at the liquor store. He said he wanted to connect people and help them. I explained that we connected people to help solve a problem for them, not to create one. That false sense of connection is a hallmark of substance use. In the beginning, people often use it as a "social lubricant" to feel less anxious or awkward in social situations. Over time all the relationships the substance promised dissolve, leaving the person more isolated than when they began using.

That night I told him that he was going to rehab, "Christopher, you're going to Tennessee. As soon as they call us to let us know there's a spot, you're going." When the conversation concluded, he agreed to go into rehab. He asked if he could have a party before he left. He wanted to have it at the bowling alley. I didn't understand why the kids wanted to do something boring like bowling. They did bowl, but they went there because they could get cigarettes out of the machine. This was when he told his friends he was going to boarding school and not the truth that he was going to rehab.

As we waited to hear back from the program in Tennessee, Chris's behavior continued to worsen. While we were on summer vacation, we received a letter notifying us that Chris would not be able to go back to the school that he loved. I remember telling him, and he cried very, very hard. He was involved there, had friends, and played sports. This was a huge blow to him, and the second time I saw him cry. He continued to use drugs even though he was losing everything he cared about. From time to time during this period, I would look at Chris, shake my head, and say, "One day we're going to get that call from Tennessee." Eventually, we did.

That fall he was enrolled at Greenville High, and that's when more trouble started to happen. He was exposed to new kids. As in any school there were a lot of good kids and a lot of bad kids. He quickly digressed.

When we finally received the call from Tennessee, we set a date for Chris's admission. On the night before Chris was scheduled to go into the program in the fall of 2000, I called him down to the den. I was naïve and had zero experience of being the father of a son who was struggling with substance use. I took a deep breath and dove in.

I looked at my son and said to him, "Christopher, you've got a problem, and we need to fix this problem in the next ninety days." Of course, at the time, I had no idea that recovery is a lifelong process, and a ninety-day "fix" is an illusion.

As we talked about entering rehab, Chris remained open to the idea of getting help. Ever the negotiator Chris said, "Dad, I'll go on one condition. Don't shut down that liquor store."

I knew the exact liquor store he was referencing. Chris continued, "I'm the only one the owner sells to. He told me that if anyone ever found out that he sold to me that he would lose his business and lose his family."

I later learned that the store owner had indeed told Chris that he was the only underage person he sold to. He then went for the emotional jugular, showing him a picture of his wife and kids and telling him that if he turned him in, he could lose his family, the store... everything. This was, of course, emotional blackmail, designed to silence a teenager, and it was effective. This secret, and a thousand more like it, create the individual strands of adolescent substance use that have captured countless teens (and communities) unaware. Honesty and active addiction are often mutually exclusive, and secrets give the disease room to grow like an unnoticed malignancy.

At that moment I was not interested in secrets. I was interested in getting my son help. I made the promise to Chris.

I went to the school to pick up Chris before leaving for Tennessee. There was a beautiful red-tailed hawk that would fly close to the school. This beautiful bird was on a bench when his school counselor met me outside. Chris came out, and we both got in the car along with Mary to head for Tennessee.

It was a long, tense drive to the program. Once we were there, a kind young man named Bob offered us lunch and allowed us to sample the food. He pointed out the gym and basketball court, which went a long way towards distracting Chris and putting him at ease. We went in and signed a litany of papers granting permission to take care of my son and help him to get well.

Finally, he was officially signed in, and it was time for us to leave.

The ride to the rehab had been tense, the trip back home was far worse. Mary was distraught, tearfully screaming for me to go back and get our son. I refused and drove us home. In a strange reversal, I was seeking to enforce limits, and Mary was struggling with being the lenient one. I've since learned that things often shift like that within a family when substance use is addressed. Our roles were changing, and there was tension at a time when we needed each other most.

At our first visit, I was eager to hear how Chris was doing. The counselor came in and after a few moments told us that Chris was doing well and asked if we had thought about what we were going to do for aftercare.

Aftercare? I should have known that this would not be as simple as "fixed in ninety days," but the idea of aftercare was a new prospect. I was starting to understand that addiction was a chronic disease, and Chris was in an acute setting. I now know that, unfortunately, many treatment centers still don't understand that distinction. I was trying to help our family survive while my son was away in rehab.

Not surprisingly, our first visit with Chris went badly. The roles continued to shift as we began to seek out a new balance in the family. Chris was angry at us for sending him there, and I was less than sympathetic to his anger. The visit essentially ended with us both angry, irritated, and frustrated. In retrospect, I think much of the impact on Chris from his time in Tennessee was the shock that we would follow through in sending him. Our interactions during visitation while he was there vacillated between his attempt to "make us pay" for sending him there and making the best of it. Other times he would attempt to turn on the charm to get something he wanted or in the hopes of getting out of treatment a little bit earlier. The visits were different in comparison to the letters he wrote to us during his time there.

Letters from Rehab

Chris wrote his first letter from rehab three days into his stay at Tennessee. I still have the letters and have re-read them many times. The opening line of the page pretty much summed up his view of how it was going:

"I just wanna let you know, this place sucks."

From that point forward, the letter explained how we were wrong for sending him to the program and how the staff there didn't know anything about him.

He explained how he was an angel compared to the other kids in the program and how they were making his problems worse. His exact words were that we had sent him to rehab "with a bunch of intravenous drug users and rednecks" and all he did was "a little weed."

He promised that now he was going to "slow down" on alcohol. Chris said that he didn't think he was addicted to marijuana, but admitted that he did abuse it. He rationalized that he didn't have to do it, but that he liked it and used it a lot.

He exclaimed that he didn't deserve to be sent there and pointed out that unlike him, all of the other kids had a record.

He said he wanted to change "some" to help himself and us.

He pointed out that he had priorities and that the other kids at the program didn't. He said that most of them had dropped out of school and that the program was a bad influence on him. He even predicted that most of the kids in the program would be in and out of jail their entire lives and that he didn't want to be around "this stuff." Ever the negotiator, Chris began at three days in asking us to consider only keeping him there for a month.

He went on to sound somewhat remorseful, saying, "I know I've caused a lot of trouble with everyone, but I wanna change all that. I'm a leader I realized, that's the difference between me and these kids, and why I've said no to a lot of stuff, well everything except pot and alcohol, because I know I'll end up liking it. That's why I've said no plenty of times."

It was not the "plenty of times" that Chris had said no that concerned me by now; it was the increased frequency with which he was saying yes. His addiction was progressively getting worse. Chris was fairly diligent in his writing to us. He began attempting to lay out the groundwork for his return home, saying "none of my friends influence me; I influence them more. I stopped letting people influence me in the 9th grade because that was part of the reason I got in trouble."

He concluded his first letter home from rehab with these words, "But oh well if you want me to be unhappy here I can't do s*** about it. I love you! Chris"

His early letters from rehab were manipulative in their attempt to convince us that he didn't have a problem. He wrote things like "I'll do marijuana, but I will stop drinking. I won't do this, but I'll still use this." The letters shifted to, "I can't do any of this stuff."

I have talked to enough parents in the years since to know this first letter home is not unique. Certain things usually happen in the first letter or phone call home from rehab that are all too common. The overall gist is that they paint the worst possible picture of the place where they are. The truth is that it could be the best program on earth, but when a young person is away from home and away from their family and friends, they tend to see it as punishment whether it's intended to be or not. Our children almost always know our fears when they go to outpatient or inpatient treatment, and they know the stereotypes and caricatures of treatment and the people in it.

They, like us, have heard the logic of "If you take kids who have a drug problem and put them with kids with other, possibly worse drug problems, why would you think they would get better?" Young people who want to get back home are all too frequently willing to play on those fears to attempt to get there.

One thing that wise programs do is to steal the thunder of the young people with a preemptive strike. They often do this by "inoculating the family" to these challenges. They tell the family up front that they may get these calls and letters and that the young person might say any number of mean and nasty things about the program. If they do, rather than rushing to pull them out of services, simply call the program or counselor and talk to them. This simple "inoculation" can save some families a world of heartache and hurt. The information braces the family for what may be early attempts to convince the family to pull them out of treatment.

The program in Tennessee didn't inoculate us at all, but we were not willing to bring Chris home at three days in or even at a month. This brings us to the second letter we received from Tennessee.

The second letter began with, "I've thought about what I wrote before to you, and I feel the same, but I decided to really focus on quitting marijuana, and I'm pretty excited about it. But I still want you to consider a month."

As Chris's brain started to clear, I caught glimpses of the boy I knew. He began to talk about his goals again. He said that he could enroll in his current high school again after Thanksgiving, but that he would only do it if he was ready. He even said that he didn't want to come home now because he knew he wasn't ready. I smiled and shook my head as I read the final lines of this letter.

"Well send me some candy and Gatorade. I love you! Chris Grant PS. Tell Kelly I love him!"

He loved us.

We loved him too.

The third letter from Tennessee came a little later on. In it he said that he was doing better and had talked to a staff member about moving to a different room where he wouldn't be around all the "wild kids" and "rednecks." He shared that he'd been thinking about how it was going to be when he got back home and was no longer "smoking weed" and getting all of "the benefits" out of it. He shared that he had talked with his counselor and had told her that he wanted our trust back. He wrote that on some nights when he had been back at home that he wasn't planning to drink but ended up drinking anyway. He even said he wanted to be able to tell us whether he was going to drink or not and that he wasn't going to keep alcohol in the house anymore unless he had to but wouldn't hide it. He said that he didn't know how he was going to quit smoking cigarettes but that he wasn't going to substitute other illegal drugs. By this time, we didn't know what to believe.

Once again, he closed the letter with:

"I love y'all" followed by a quick "Oh yeah! Can you get me a Gameboy, and Tetris and other "phat" games, because anything that'll make time go by I'll do. Please! Just get Kelly to help you with the games. Well I love you! Chris

P.S. Gatorade Please!"

What a strange juxtaposition it was. In my mind, we were fighting to get our son back, and he was focused on getting a video game. Still, I was hopeful. Yes, glimmers of Chris were coming back to the surface, and I felt as though just maybe we were getting our baby boy back again.

When someone stops using, the brain conditions away from drug and alcohol use, the longer they are away from the drugs, the clearer their thinking becomes. The brain is literally creating new neurotransmitters. They no longer think about drugs every second as they do when they first arrive at rehab. The change is apparent with a brain scan after 30 days of abstinence. Chris's letters reflected that.

The content changed from telling me I was crazy for sending him there to saying it was the best thing I ever did for him.

The age of first use is a big indicator of one's ability to maintain sobriety. Statistically, the younger they start, the less likely they are to remain sober. Insurance companies often dictate twenty-eight-day programs. On average, adults try seven times before they have sobriety. That's why it fascinates me when I meet someone that says they went one time and never used again. I wonder if they had a problem with addiction or if they were depressed. Rarely, but every so often I do hear someone say they did it on their own, like my uncle.

Read 1rst

Dear Mom & Dad,

I just wanna let you know, this place sucks. You told they were going to talk to me to see how big my problem is, well its been three days, and they don't know crap about me. I've figured out some things since I've been here: I'm a angel compared to the kids here, I think they are just making my problems worse. They are all pretty much dumb loud rednecks. That drank everyday, and have done just about everything. They are so annoying.

Early letters from teens in rehab often start like this. It is seldom that adolescents are excited about being away from home. Even if it is to help them get healthy, they often feel like it is punitive. Families need to know that if a teen goes into treatment, they almost certainly won't say thank you, at least not at first.

Read 2nd

Dear Mom & Dad,

I've thought about what I wrote before to you, and I feel the same, but I decided to really focus on quitting marijuana, and I'm pretty excited about it. But I still want you to consider a month. I can enroll to Greenvill high after Thanksgiving. But I'll only do it if I'm ready. And I don't want to come home now, b/c I know I'm not ready. Well send me some candy and gatorades.

I ♡ U !

PS Tell Kelly I ♡ him!

This second letter begins to show how Chris had started to consider making some changes. He even went as far as to say he knows he wasn't ready to come home yet.

Dear Mom & Dad,

What's up? I'm doing better. I talked to Bob today about moving me to a different room where I wouldn't be around all these wild kids He's working on it. But I'm excited about seeing you next sunday. I've been thinking about how it's gonna be when I get back and not smoking weed, and all the benifits I will get out of it, I had an individual meeting w/ Miss Kathy and she asked me all these questions and I was very honest w/ her. She said I was dependent on weed, and I didn't ha

The bad news is that substance use is often progressive, but the good news is that so is recovery. By this time in his treatment, I was beginning to see glimpses of my son coming back to me.

All I Do is a Little Weed

Chris minimized his drug use. As I mentioned before from his letters, he'd often say things like, "All I do is a little weed."

Few behaviors characterize active substance use like minimization and rationalizing. Often, when a person is asked about their drug use, they will respond with one of these two ways. In Chris's case, I heard both.

Minimizing is when someone seeks to make their use seem less impactful or significant than it is. When Chris arrived at rehab, he did not embrace it with open arms. Most teenagers don't. His first letter home explained how much he hated where he was. He found a million things to complain about, but probably one of the things that was clearest in his letter was how much "worse" the other kids there were than he was. After all, he just used "a little weed," and these were "intravenous drug users." In this way, he downplayed and minimized his use.

This is where minimization's cousin, rationalization, often comes in.

For instance, often those who drink will rationalize "at least what I use is legal."

Those using marijuana often reason "what I use is organic and comes from the earth."

Those using cocaine may suggest that "at least cocaine isn't as bad as meth."

Often those using opiates justify "I get my drugs from a pharmacy" or "at least I don't shoot up."

In short, the tendency is to believe that whatever substance one uses is somehow better than the substances others use. The truth is although the potency may vary, all drugs of abuse impact the same dopaminergic, survival pathway in the brain. Society may deem one drug as better or worse than another, but biology does not.

In Chris's case, he painted those in the rehab with him in as negative of a light possible. He derided their intelligence, claimed they were on harder drugs than he had ever done, and predicted that all of them would probably end up going in and out of prison throughout their lives. Such statements are common, but they are often inaccurate. When a person is somewhere that they don't want to be, they often attempt to find a way to be elsewhere. Chris knew we cared about who he associated with, and he knew we valued education and sought to avoid legal entanglements. He knew that bringing these things up would make it harder for us to believe that rehab was the best place for him.

Ultimately, it didn't work. Chris remained at the rehab and eventually completed the treatment program. His minimizing his struggles with substance use didn't stop there. I was afraid that the drugs would keep using him, my amazing son, until he was all used up. In retrospect, I can see that my expectations for the program in Tennessee were unrealistic because they were treating a chronic disease in an acute setting; I felt like treatment had not worked.

Some people believe that marijuana is a gateway drug. The research indicates that this is true for some people but not everyone. I only know it was true for Chris. It was not only the gateway to using other drugs; it was also a gateway to some of the predictions he made about those in his first rehab coming true in his own life. His using "just a little weed" eventually turned into using more drugs.

Aftercare and the Abbeville Experiment

As Chris began to progress towards completing the program, the counselor continued to talk with us about aftercare, and it became increasingly clear that Chris's friends at his current high school were not going to be cheerleaders for his sobriety. Many of them believed that he was at a fancy boarding school and would send him letters adorned with pictures of joints and blunts telling him he would be "back in the saddle again soon." After a lot of thinking and soul-searching, we decided to ask my parents if Chris could stay with them in Abbeville County when he came home. They would have done anything for Chris; though apprehensive, they agreed. How long he would be there was uncertain; so, I agreed to send money to help offset the costs of his being there, and our aftercare plan was in motion. I went to see Chris at least four nights a week, which further strained my marriage and gave me less time to spend with my younger son, Kelly.

One question that loomed with his moving to a new county was where to enroll him in school. I knew that drugs could be prevalent in any school, but I thought that Chris's odds might be better at a private school. There were only two private schools in the area. When I went to enroll Chris in a new school, I was not aware of the possibility of what would happen next.

I visited a private school in Greenwood, SC with the intent to explain Chris's circumstances and to enroll him in school. I answered the questions honestly, careful to highlight the good and the bad. After the interview, I met with a school administrator. I was informed that they would not accept Chris. I was stunned. I had been in sales my entire life, and fortunately, I had always had the privilege of selling excellent products and services. I slowly began to realize that day as I was attempting to "sell' the enrollment of my son to the school, that in their eyes, I was selling damaged goods. They didn't want him there. I went out to my car, got in, and wept with my head on the steering wheel.

I sat in my car lost in my thoughts. The tap on the window from an administrator startled me. He came out to tell me that he was sorry for the answer they had to give. He then shared some personal information with me. He said that he could not tell me in front of the other staff inside, but that he was a recovering heroin addict. He said that he understood how difficult this must be, but that he had to protect the other kids in the school.

Although heartbroken, I understood his dilemma and considered his telling me his story an act of kindness. Here I saw a person who had used drugs who was by all accounts doing well in a respected role in a community. On the other hand, he felt the need to hide his past use, even from those who entrusted their children to his care.

The other private school in the area likewise declined to admit Chris. We chose the only other option we were aware of and enrolled him in Abbeville High School. When Chris arrived on the scene as a new student, as is often the case in rural schools, he received a lot of attention. Chris was an athletic, good-looking kid. His first day at the school he joined junior varsity basketball and met a pretty, young lady. When I spoke with him that afternoon, he announced to me that he "had the best day of his life." I almost jumped through the ceiling with excitement for him! I was hopeful that this could be a turning point for him. Finally, just maybe, he had found his niche, and things would begin to turn around.

Chris began dating the "pretty, young lady" shortly after he started attending the school. She was by all accounts beautiful and bright, and she happened to be the daughter of a conservative pastor in the area. Chris continued to play sports and spent time with friends playing basketball. It seemed like maybe things were going to keep getting better. I still drove to Abbeville to see Chris four nights a week. He began attending outpatient treatment at a local agency three nights per week. My father often took him there, and his counselor was a serious, supportive man.

Things seemed to be looking up for Chris. We were getting into a new rhythm, but that rhythm was short-lived. My first indication that things might not be as good as they seemed was when I learned Chris was taking an over-the-counter nasal decongestant. If one has a cold or allergies that may not be such a big deal. Chris was using them in amounts that made no sense to me.

Shortly after I learned about his using the over-the-counter medication, my parents found marijuana in his room.

Chris started getting in some other trouble. His relationship with the young lady imploded quickly. He received several tickets in town for playing loud music in his car. This was probably in part due to his choice of music. Abbeville was a town that was racially divided during this time. Chris had friends of every race, and some of his music choices probably did not sit too well with the local authorities. That said, it could not all be chalked up to racial tensions. Chris received an open container charge while living in Abbeville county. In fact, he received three. I had a friend who was an attorney in Abbeville, and he helped me to mitigate those charges. I was doing everything that I knew how to do to try to keep him from self-destructing and cutting his own legs out from under him.

Some people call that enabling. I called it loving my son and helping him as best as I knew how.

Others also looked out for him. For instance, Chris did catch a break when he was pulled over after attending a party in an adjacent town. Chris was under the influence and had allowed a fourteen-year-old to drive his car while he was rolling joints in the passenger seat. When my dad and I arrived at the scene where he had been pulled over, I figured Chris was done for and prepared for the worst. Instead, the state trooper who had pulled him over confided to me that he had a son who was "just like mine" and was going through some of the same things. He let him go.

The stress on my parents during this time was tremendous. They were unaccustomed to all of the turmoil that comes with having a person in active addiction in the home with them. It was quickly becoming clear that Chris's Abbeville experiment had not worked as we had hoped.

I tried to limit the casualties along the way. Unfortunately, I couldn't protect my mother. She had a psychotic episode after Chris stayed with them in Abbeville. I had never seen anyone in her condition. We took her to a local psychiatric hospital. My mother was babbling; she couldn't take the stress anymore. That was a difficult time. I had been driving to Abbeville several times a week just to visit and oversee Chris while he was staying with my parents.

In Between

Following the troubles in Abbeville, Mary and I began to realize that Chris was going to need more than family support to maintain his sobriety. We took him to a local psychiatric hospital for stabilization. Chris returned home with me in Greenville and enrolled in outpatient services at another treatment agency. He also enrolled in classes for ADSAP (our state's driver's license re-licensure program). Things were not going well. He was using drugs and the relationships between Chris, Mary, and I continued to deteriorate.

The culmination of this deterioration occurred on an evening when Chris was using profanity and being verbally abusive towards Mary. This was partially set in motion because I had broken the lock on a footlocker in his room. Inside I found lots of pornography and an inordinate amount of loose tobacco. Although I didn't know it at the time, I later understood that this was from his cutting open cigars to roll marijuana "blunts" in the cigar paper. He was furious that I had opened the footlocker and directed his anger at Mary. I intervened, and before I knew what happened, Chris and I were tussling on the floor. Up until this point, our family had absolutely no history of abuse or violence of any kind, and this event was sobering to me. Chris was a lot stronger than I anticipated, and it was not a quick altercation. We locked up physically downstairs and throughout the course of the skirmish made our way upstairs to his room. Kelly kept screaming, "Dad, you're going to have a heart attack!" as he tried to intervene to break us apart. I did not have a heart attack, but I did experience a tremendous heartbreak. After that night, I began seeking out longer, more comprehensive options for Chris.

One of the places I found was a boarding school in Arden, NC. As before, I went and talked with the people who ran the school regarding admission, and just as before I was told he would not be accepted. In their words, "He isn't ready for us yet," meaning he would need to be more stable in order to enter their school.

It was during this time that I solicited the help of a friend of mine who was a detective. I had no idea what to do, but I knew that Chris needed help and that something had to change. I was desperate, and I asked my friend to talk to Chris in the hopes it would scare the crap out of him. He agreed and arrived one evening and asked to speak to Chris. He talked with Chris for about an hour that evening. Then I held my breath and waited. If anything, Chris's use seemed to escalate after that meeting. At that time, I didn't know anything about programs designed to scare someone into sobriety and their poor success rates. If fear were a sufficient motivator to get and keep people in recovery, then few people who are addicted would still be using. I didn't know all of that then. I only saw that Chris's use seemed more invigorated after that meeting. As parents, we do the best we know how to do for our children at the time. Unfortunately, in this case, and many others, it simply was not enough and did not work out like we hoped it would.

After some further searching, I found a treatment program in Hattiesburg, Mississippi. This was the same rehabilitation program that had treated several famous individuals. A physician friend of mine sent his son to the program and offered to let me speak with him. His son and I met, and he shared with me about his time there and how the program worked. Feeling some reassurance following our conversation, I decided to pursue it for Chris.

The program was expensive, at that time about $27,000 per month, but for Chris, we would make a way. As we arrived on campus, I noticed how beautiful the grounds were. I felt good about Chris being somewhere nice for treatment. By now, Chris was over sixteen years old, but we had some legal sway over him since he was a minor. The strain in our marriage had taken a toll. Mary and I were separated by this time; so, I took Chris to the facility on my own. After enrolling him and paying the first installment, I felt anxious, but I had some sense of relief. I don't know if most parents of someone struggling with substance use ever fully feel at ease, but I at least felt better than I had. I knew Chris's battle with addiction was taking a toll on me. I took a few days off from work and took a long route home passing through Tupelo, Mississippi and the Florida Panhandle. Chris was at the program in Hattiesburg for right at ninety days before successfully completing services.

Initially he wanted to remain in their aftercare program, which was usually about thirty to ninety days. Ultimately, he decided that he wanted to leave after just one week and returned home to live with me. Not surprisingly we learned that he had begun using again shortly thereafter when he tested positive for marijuana.

Although I did not know it at the time, I later learned that my friend's son had already relapsed by the time that he and I met to discuss the program. He told me this later on and expressed how terrible he felt about it. Today he is married and is doing well in active recovery. There is a high recurrence, or relapse, rate following treatment for substance use. Knowing that fact did not make it hurt any less.

When Chris came home from rehab this time, I was unsure which way to go. The program in Hattiesburg had taken an emotional toll, as well as a financial toll, and I was half-broke. We had no idea what to do about his schooling, and I had no idea what to do in general. People kept telling me that he needed something longer term, eighteen months or so. I began researching different options again and, after digging through every program I could find, came back to the boarding school in Arden, NC. I knew some of the kids who had gone there reportedly had a "checkered past," and I thought the school was more of a therapeutic boarding school. Maybe this longer-term approach would make the difference. Perhaps, with his having gone through the Hattiesburg program, he would be stable enough to get in.

Chris agreed to go to the school, and this time, the school accepted him. The tuition for the school at that time was about $40,000 per year, not counting any of the "soft costs" or extras that arise. I recall asking how people could afford such a place and was told: "there are kids here whose parents don't have two nickels to rub together and there are some kids' parents that could write a check for the entire school!" I told him that we were closer to the first group of parents who didn't have two nickels to rub together. Our resources were extremely lean from Chris's time in Hattiesburg, but if the school in Arden could help Chris get back on track and help us get our son back, it would be worth it. We would figure it out.

Chris integrated into life at the school fairly quickly. He was kicking on their football team and later began playing soccer. Chris had a strong foot. He was a talented soccer player, and he could also kick a football into the end zone that couldn't be returned. He made some friends while he was there in the school. Unfortunately, not all of those friends were interested in Chris's sobriety.

One of the nuances of this particular school was that when a student got in trouble there, their restitution was to cut down a tree and then dig up the stump using only a shovel and a pickaxe. He was at the school on September 11, 2001. I explained what had happened with the terrorist attack and the twin towers. He made it through the first year, his junior year, but during the year he had managed to get on probation at the school for bringing alcohol on campus.

When he came home that summer, he worked at a clothing store in the mall. Unfortunately, part of his motivation for working was to have money to support his substance use. Not surprisingly, it did not take long before Chris quit showing up for work and he was let go from the job. Of course, we didn't know that until we went by the store to check in on him one day and were told by his manager that he had been fired two weeks before.

Some people in our neighborhood knew Chris, neighbors you would never suspect, used substances. Some even came over to ostensibly visit or to "borrow the bathroom" to look for drugs in our home. These individuals were just as likely to be adults as they were teenagers. Chris was extremely sexually active during this time, and not surprisingly, many of his encounters and relationships involved drugs on some level. Like many who are actively using substances, Chris had fallen victim to the belief that relationships could be cultivated and grown through substance use. In the end, that is always a bait and switch scheme.

The drug use took away the relationships that it had promised with interest.

When summer ended, Chris returned to school in Arden as a senior. It did not take long for the start of the year to get rocky. He got caught with marijuana and faced the choice between being kicked out directly or becoming a boarding student. Since the school was in NC and I lived in SC, I did the only thing I could think of at the time. I reserved a room at a Holiday Inn near the school for a month. So, in addition to the school expense, Chris was now a "town" student commuting in from the Holiday Inn. Within a month, Chris was caught bringing alcohol on campus and was kicked out for good. He later told me that although he had made many screw ups over the years, one of his biggest regrets was not taking advantage of the opportunity he had while at the school.

Shortly after Chris was kicked out, I received a bill via certified mail totaling $18,000 for the remainder of his tuition minus the tuition insurance I bought up-front.

I later learned that most people there bought the tuition replacement, meaning that if the student left the school or did not make it through the year that some of the tuition would be covered. In retrospect, that should have been some indication of the success rate of the school. Chris did not complete the semester, and I wrestled with whether or not to pay the bill. I had the funds to cover it, but barely. Writing an $18,000 check for an education that my son would not even be able to receive was no easy task and from a fiscal standpoint was a hard pill to swallow. I contacted the school and essentially settled with them for $8,000 rather than the $18,000 owed. Writing that check was one of the hardest financial things that I had ever done. The check sat in my desk drawer for a week before I finally convinced myself to send it to the school. I still have a coffee cup I received from the school at the start of Chris's senior year there. I call it my $80,000 coffee cup.

It's Not Always as It Seems

One of the challenges of youth is learning to see life as it is and not as people portray it. For adolescents, this means that there is often a learning curve as they discover that not everything is as simple and straightforward as they believed in childhood. We lived in a relatively nice neighborhood during the boys' early teen years, and they both went to private schools. At times, our boys (especially Chris) would think that other families had a perfect life. Someone in the neighborhood's son or daughter might get a new car, a new game, or new "toy" of some kind, and they would think this meant all was well within their family.

From time-to-time, when Chris would head down this mental path, I would look at him and say, "It's not always as it seems." Like much of parenting, you're not always sure if your children are getting the meaning of the messages you are seeking to convey. In this case, Chris did.

During this time, another couple about our age would often invite our family, as well as other families, over to their home on Friday evenings. They were wonderful people and gracious hosts and were known to be wealthy. They would laugh and seemed to enjoy entertaining the many visitors that came. At one point, the relationship exploded and resulted in a nasty split and divorce. Chris looked at me one night as we were leaving and said, "Dad, can you keep a secret?" Not sure where this was going, I said, "Can you?" He said that the son of the couple we had just been visiting had told him that his parents were getting a divorce. I glanced back at Chris and asked, "Do you know what that is?" I will never forget Chris looking at me with a sad wisdom beyond his years and saying, "It is not always as it seems."

The need to keep up appearances is alive and well among all people, but it particularly thrives where status is valued. Unfortunately, these appearances are often a death sentence for many. I advocated for my children consistently. I did not go out of my way to air their dirty laundry; at the same time, desperation pushed me beyond my desire for pretense. I wanted to help Chris get better more than I wanted to pretend to have it all together.

Chris vacillated on how open he was with sharing his struggles. On the one hand, I heard him correct an older gentleman at church one day who asked how he had enjoyed his time away at school. Chris told him that he hadn't been in school but that he had been at a rehab. When the gentleman asked what sort of injury he was going to rehab for, Chris explained that it was a drug rehab. On the other hand, at times I would hear a comment from someone (often an attractive young lady's mother) that seemed to indicate Chris was at a boarding school somewhere. In his way, I think Chris was working through the desire to be honest about his need for help versus the stigma he knew he would encounter if people knew he was using.

This stigma leads many families to ignore and cover-up substance abuse and problems in the home rather than to be honest about their struggles and reach out for help. This contributes to the familial isolation that is one of the main calling cards of addiction.

The stereotype of a person with a substance use disorder has historically been someone who was weak-willed, dirty, homeless, toothless, a criminal, unkempt, poor, mentally unstable, and a host of other negative associations. The truth is that about one in ten people will struggle with a substance use disorder in their lifetime and the description above accounts for only a tiny fraction of this population. This matters to me profoundly because it is this view of what it means to have a substance use disorder that keeps many who need help from getting the help they need.

The logic goes that if someone with a drug problem is homeless around a fire barrel under the overpass and that description does not describe my current circumstances, then clearly, I don't need the help. There is the idea of this mystical "hitting bottom" that is pervasive even in parts of the recovery community. The problem with waiting on a loved one to "hit bottom" is that some amazing people break when they land. Some do not make it back and some will die.

What other diseases would we choose to wait until it became as dire as possible before treating? We seek to identify problems early with heart disease, hypertension, and diabetes and to then intervene. Can you imagine saying to someone whose blood pressure was high, "Why don't we wait until you hit bottom by having a stroke? Then you'll be ready to receive some help!" That would be ludicrous. That mindset is pervasive when it comes to substance use disorders.

Most people who have a substance use disorder have no clue that they have one. This is not because they are in denial; it is because they have a misunderstanding of what a substance use disorder "looks like." When they expect the homeless man to struggle with addiction, it is easy to miss the businessman who is struggling. When they expect the prostitute to struggle with addiction, it is easy to miss the housewife who is struggling. It is an insidious lie that says to someone that it is more important to keep up the appearance of health than it is to be healthy. If by some miracle we do manage to keep up that appearance, and then we die young related to substance use, I suppose people may speak well of us at our funeral. Sadly, that is little consolation to the loved ones left behind.

We all like to pretend we have all of our stuff together, but the truth is that none of us do. The truth is that it really is not always what it seems.

Let's be courageous enough to be vulnerable and not drown because we are too proud to raise our hand as we go under. Let's learn to see past the stereotypes of addiction to the reality of it. For instance, the actual symptoms beyond the stereotypes include things like tolerance, failure to fulfill major roles, unsuccessful attempts to cut down or quit using, cravings, spending a lot of time related to the substance, taking the substance longer or in larger amounts than intended, and other hard-to-spot behaviors. One of the main challenges of acknowledging a need for help is that the stereotypes of use are often easy to spot, but the actual symptoms are not. Helping others understand what substance use disorders look like can be a tremendous step in the right direction.

For Chris, I had ringside seats to his fight for recovery. I was close enough to see the toll his use was taking on him, and it frightened me.

Cried Three Times

Drugs have a way of blunting the emotions of those who use them in many ways. As Glenn Frey and Don Henley of the Eagles wrote:

"You're losing all your highs and lows.

Ain't it funny how the feeling goes away."

This was certainly true of Chris during his use. Throughout all of his struggles, I only ever saw him cry three times.

I have already mentioned the first two. I saw Chris cry when he wrecked and totaled his car. He had left the counseling office angry and ended up having an accident. Maybe it was partly the adrenalin, or perhaps it was genuine remorse, but he cried when I arrived, and we embraced each other. He cried when he learned that he was not going to be able to return to his old high school. Chris was involved at school. He was playing sports and knew the people there. When he found out that he wouldn't be able to return, he cried hard.

The third time that I saw Chris cry came on a particularly difficult day when he was screaming at his mother. In the midst of the chaos I told him that I didn't know who he was anymore. It was the truth. This sweet, generous, compassionate child that I loved had changed. He had become angry, selfish, and dishonest. He was cruel to his mother and lashed out at those who loved him most. This is because drugs are thieves. They steal time, money, relationships, esteem, and even personal identity from those who use them. The drugs were stealing his emotions from him and were trying to steal my son from me.

One of the struggles for many people in early recovery is that they begin to feel again. Often, they have been running an emotional tab of pain for years or even decades. When they quit using, their emotions are often raw and come screaming back online with a vengeance. Without developing some good coping skills and support quickly, a person is almost doomed to have a recurrence of symptoms. Crying is a good thing when a person is hurting. That Chris cried so little probably says more about his use than his tears would have.

Likewise, there is a strong correlation between substance use and trauma. The short version is that those with trauma in their backgrounds are more likely to use substances. The vicious cycle is that those who use substances are more likely to be re-traumatized. Although, as far as I know, Chris had no specific trauma in his history, the progression of his addiction was beginning to yield more traumatic consequences for both him and our family.

The Worst 28 Days

Over the years, as is often true of siblings of those who use substances, Kelly got neglected as we sought to handle Chris's addiction. It was not, of course, intentional. We loved both boys the same, but when a child is in crisis, whether it is addiction or heart disease, they tend to absorb the attention of the family. Kelly was a brilliant full moon who got lost in the blazing sun of Chris's addiction. I did not see this at the time, but I see it clearly in retrospect.

This can be seen on one occasion when Kelly was completing the eighth grade. He won many awards at the close of the school year and was incredibly excited and, rightly, proud of his accomplishments. After receiving his awards at the ceremony, he returned to his classroom where students were to pick up their report cards. Instead of a report card, Kelly received a letter. He received this letter because I had not paid his last month's tuition for the school year yet. The irony was that I was Chairman of the Board of the school at the time. Even so, much of the family's finances had gone into Chris's rehabs and I simply couldn't make the payment for Kelly's school. Kelly was devastated and angry, and he had every right to be. Nonetheless, it was not the last time my attention on Chris would prevent me from being the father I wanted to be for Kelly.

The clearest example of Kelly not getting his due attention occurred during a time where, ironically, I was intentionally trying to spend more time with him.

I decided to take Kelly and a couple of his friends on a cruise following his high school graduation in 2004. This was a Mediterranean cruise and would mean that we would be gone for over two weeks together, a chance to spend some good, focused time with my youngest son. I was looking forward to spending some time with him and his friends and celebrating together. I confess to being nervous about leaving Chris alone for that long. That fear turned out to be founded.

Towards the end of the cruise, I began getting emails from Mary about Chris. Keep in mind that during this time, getting emails on a cruise was a novelty and was an expensive venture. What unfolded through the emails was that Chris had gotten arrested for public drunkenness and was sentenced to twenty-eight days in jail.

Earlier that evening, Chris and his girlfriend had been spoken to by the arresting officer for causing a disturbance. Chris was clearly under the influence, but when the officer realized that he lived close to where he was, he decided to "cut him a break." He told Chris to walk straight home and that he had "bigger fish to fry" that evening. Chris did go straight home. When he arrived, he was no less impaired. He began to yell and scream and became aggressive toward Mary. Mary believed Chris was going to hurt her and called the police. When the officers responded, Chris was arrested for "public drunkenness."

From the moment I became aware of Chris's arrest, my attention was split, and I was distracted for the remainder of the trip. Even when I was physically present with Kelly, I wasn't fully present with him. Here I was, on a cruise to spend time with my youngest son, and my attention was suddenly back on my oldest. Even from the ship I began trying to reach out for legal help and to do what I could to get him out of jail. The judge wanted to be firm with Chris and to make an example of him. Despite my writing to the judge and trying to contact him, Chris was required to serve the entire twenty-eight days. Although in retrospect, I believe the judge was truly trying to help Chris, this was the longest twenty-eight days of my life. Ironically, the judge's wife had been one of Chris and Kelly's preschool teachers.

When I arrived back home, one of the first things I did was to appear with Chris at his hearing. It is a surreal experience to see your child brought into the courtroom in an orange jumpsuit and handcuffs. The sight of it stunned me.

I honestly think that both he and his girlfriend believed he would get to come home with me after the hearing because I knew the judge. I hoped that would be the case, and I guess some part of me believed he would be released. Chris was sentenced at the end of the hearing. The bailiff immediately led my son out of the courtroom away from me. I will never forget the sight of him being taken away in handcuffs and a jail uniform.

To my dismay, I couldn't save him from the consequences of his actions that day, but that did not keep me from continuing to try. Over the next few weeks, I continued to attempt to reach out to the judge and do everything in my power to get him released, but it was to no avail. This meant that for a couple of weeks I was only able to speak to my son through safety glass. There is only so much to talk about via phone through glass for an hour at a time. It wasn't just awkward. To see him there and be unable to make it better, to be unable to do anything for him or to even hug him, was one of the most powerless feelings I had experienced up until that point. I visited him every day and feel like I probably lost several years off of my own life during that month.

In recovery circles for addiction, powerlessness is talked about a lot. Few people realize that powerlessness is just as big of a challenge to the family who loves someone who is addicted. This was a defining point in my coming to understand once again that I could not save Chris. I did not realize it yet, but I was even more powerless than I realized.

Though no one can go back and make a brand new start my friend, anyone can start from now and make a brand new end.

CARL BARD

One of the ways I attempted to support Chris in his recovery was by giving him gifts that were positive and encouraging. This hung on his bathroom mirror for many years.

Houston, We Have Liftoff

I was at a loss.

Chris was continuing to use, and I had no idea what to try next. I was coming to realize that the changes that Chris needed to make would probably take months to accomplish. Our resources were all but depleted, and our emotional resources were even emptier. Nonetheless, I was determined to do what I could do to help my son. After some looking and investigation, I found a program in Houston, Texas. This particular program cost $9,000 per month. I took Chris there and wrote out a check for the first month, having no idea how I was going to cover it and keenly aware that the program was scheduled to last seventeen more months. I recall that the program was down a long, dirt road. There were several big guys there as I checked Chris in, and I got the impression that they would help ensure that he would be staying. It was quite a way out from town, and I got a little turned around in the dark on the way back to the hotel. When I finally did make it back to the hotel and had gotten settled in, there was a knock at the door. It was Chris.

He must have left just after I did. Chris had hitched a ride and had probably beaten me back to the hotel. I am fairly certain that he had seen me come in and waited until I was in the room before he came and knocked on the door shortly after my arrival.

I couldn't believe my eyes. "Christopher, what are you doing here?"

"I am not doing that program, Dad. Those kids are crazy!"

I had no idea what to do. He was no longer considered a minor by this point, but he was still my son. I had exhausted every resource I had as well as some that I did not to try to help him. I was completely unable to save him from himself and this disease that had taken over my firstborn baby. At this moment, I did one of the hardest things I have ever done in my life. I looked at my son and told him,

"Christopher, I have one ticket home. Here is $20. You can use it to eat tonight or to get drugs, but I won't be taking you home." I don't know which one he decided to do that night. I got on the plane and left him on the streets of Houston.

The flight home was excruciating. I didn't second-guess myself; I quadruple-guessed myself. I wanted help for Chris, but I was coming to understand that it was beyond my power to give it to him. I cried nearly the entire flight. The collar of my shirt was damp. If tears could save a person from addiction, we wouldn't have an epidemic in this country.

Chris was, nonetheless, incredibly resourceful. I later learned that he spent a week on the streets of Houston before finally finding and connecting with a distant relative there, an ex-spouse of an in-law. Chris had her son's number in his cell phone, and they knew each other, but they were far from close.

It turned out her son was not only into drugs but also criminal activity. While Chris was there, he began using heavier drugs and got deeper into dealing. Not surprisingly, he wound up being arrested there. Things were not going well for him.

Déjà vu

Chris stayed in Houston for about six months in all, living with this relative and her son. As a way of supporting them in looking after Chris during this time, I sent them $600 per month. He enrolled in school there, but his academics weren't going well either. He continued using and dealing drugs, and the son of the relative and Chris seemed to be fueling each other's downward spiral.

By the end of the six months, and with the new additional arrest there, Chris returned home from Houston. The simple truth was that he had worn out his welcome there. I paid for him to fly back home to

Greenville, but I had no delusions that he would be able to just come home and make it.

Even though this was a dark time overall, we did have some small victories.

Chris had attended five different high schools, not counting the rehab programs he had been enrolled in.

Despite this, Chris had not managed to earn his diploma. Once Chris was back home, I took him to the small town of Camden, South Carolina, on a sweltering hot day to take his GED test. He passed and received his GED in the mail about three weeks later. He was proud of it and couldn't wait to show his brother. I was excited too and hoped that maybe this would help him to get a little traction and turn the corner with regards to his use and his goals.

Chris enrolled in a local technical college in the fall of 2003. Although he was in school, Chris was continuing to struggle heavily with his drug use. Not surprisingly, his drug use had not improved his study habits. I know now that even when he was trying his best, his drug use impaired his ability to learn. The reality is that a person who is actively using may function and be incredibly intelligent, but they will not be able to function optimally or be as intelligent as they would have been without the drug. This is one more way using alcohol and other drugs steals from the person using. At the end of Chris's inaugural semester, he had a grade point average of zero. He had failed every course. He still persevered and wanted to get a degree. I saved a few of the papers he wrote during this time; they give me a glimpse of his thoughts. In October 2004, Chris wrote a paper on the book *Who Moved My Cheese*. A few things that he wrote cast some light on the fact that he was struggling against the disease of addiction:

"Some learn to be successful, and some learn the hard way. I can identify with Hem a lot in this story. I find myself looking in wrong places for my cheese. I find myself waiting on good things to happen instead of going out and making things happen by acting. I also find myself scared to go out and take risks. My fears hold me back from being successful."

"My cheese is being clean and happy. I struggle with being happy and wait around for it like Hem did, and when I do that I get miserable."

"Sometimes in my life I just go with the flow like the mice did."

"It taught me not to give up and gave me hope in my future."

Chris wanted to get better. One key point of anyone struggling with their substance use is that they are *struggling* with it. Chris knew that he was going to have to do something in order to recover; he could not be passive and wait for recovery to come to him.

After talking it over further, Chris and I decided that he would return to the program in Hattiesburg. Keep in mind that by this time, Chris was an adult. I couldn't make him go anywhere. Chris believed that the program in Hattiesburg was good; since he was willing to go, I worked out the arrangements for him to return.

At one point while in the program for the second time, I recall Chris telling me many things he was sorry for during a family day. By this time, Mary and I had already long since been separated and were going through a divorce. It was during this second time in Mississippi that we attended a family day with Chris. He was sharing with the group the things that he had done and the substances he had used. After he finished sharing what he felt remorseful for, a young lady spoke up. I will never forget the words that she said. "I'm going to have to call bulls*** on that. Chris, I think you're just a drug addict on training wheels."

At that moment, the hair on the back of my neck raised. In retrospect, her words had the ring of prophecy to them.

1-26-01

Chris -
Please read.
Great message that
applies to my love
and hope for
you. I love you.
I am proud of
you. Keep making
decisions that are
in your best interest.
Love,
Dad

FRIDAY •

God Is

Read

There is nothing
be able to separate 1
is ours through Chr
— Ro

*W*hen I was a bc
storm windows and scr
our house. In the sprin
storm windows and ins
procedure was reversed
second floor that could
When it was time to ch
hold on to my ankles a
window, unhook the sc
hand it in to my brothe
window 20 feet above t
that my father who lov
ankles, and he would n
The years that follov
difficult and sometime:
Father who loves me ha
never let go. That pror
again by God's firm bu

Prayer: Loving God, w
frightening, remind us
see us through. We res
care. Amen.

Thou
God who love

30 *Prayer Focus:* PEO\

I was constantly trying to think of things that would encourage and support Christopher in his recovery. This is another example of something meaningful that I gave to Chris. It hung on his bathroom mirror during the time he lived with me.

The Death of a Son

Chris only stayed in Hattiesburg for about thirty days before leaving. Once again, he returned home and was living with me. By this time, our divorce was being finalized after nearly twenty-five years of marriage. Our relationship was, in part, collateral damage to the addiction.

Chris was struggling on all fronts by this time. In the fall semester of 2005, he wrote up a plan of things he needed to do in order to get back on track in school. His plan included things like going to bed and getting up at the right hour, getting enough sleep, and taking his prescribed medications. He acknowledged that he needed to take his ADHD medication every day to help him focus. Chris shared that he needed to make a schedule and keep up with when and where his classes were held.

In September of 2005, Chris wrote an essay on the impact of alcohol on people's lives. He wrote, "Addiction is a disease. In some cases, it might run in the family history." If knowledge of a disease was enough to stop one from having it, then we could educate ourselves into health. This is not true for cancer, hypertension, or diabetes, and it is not true of addiction. You cannot out-educate an illness.

By this time, Chris was once again using and selling. Even so, he was still my son. You don't stop loving your child just because they are sick. You might be angry, frustrated, and hurt at times, but you love them nonetheless. He remained enrolled in school at the technical college. He was living with me and was working with me at the office so that I could help keep an eye on him and try to be a support to him.

On Sunday, October 16, 2005, I looked into Chris's room to check in on him before going to sleep myself for the night. A friend of his had visited him earlier in the day, and I wanted to make sure that he was ok. That's just the sort of thing a father does. Chris was lying on the floor, sound asleep and snoring. Although he didn't usually snore to speak of, Chris fell asleep on the floor all the time; so, I didn't think much of it. I turned in to get some rest.

I learned later that snoring can be indicative of an overdose which can cause breathing to slow. The snoring may have an almost guttural sound to it. This is because the size of the airway is reduced and not as much air can move in and out of the lungs with each breath. If I had known then what I know now, I would have tried to wake him that night.

Unknown to me at the time, the friend who had visited with Chris earlier in the day had been providing him with methadone pills to sell. The night that Chris died, he had used cocaine. He probably used the methadone pills to come down from the cocaine he had taken and then nodded off to sleep on the floor.

The next morning when I went to wake Chris up, he was still on the floor. I went over and reached out my hand to wake him. He was cold to the touch.

Chris looked peaceful, almost like he was sleeping. I knew better. My son was gone.

I can't explain what I did next.

In the face of finding my son dead on the floor, I went and began to brush my teeth to go to work. Therapists might say that I was in shock, and I'd be hard-pressed to argue with them. My amazing, compassionate, athletic son was gone.

Chris died on October 17, 2005, less than a month after writing the essay I mentioned previously on alcohol. He was twenty-one years old. At that point, as far as I knew, I had never met a single person who had lost a child to an overdose. I felt hollow and incredibly, unbearably alone.

OPINION

Christopher Robert Grant, a 21 year old white male, died as a result of mixed drug (cocaine and methadone) intoxication. He was reportedly found dead by his father when he tried to wake him in the morning for school. His past social history is significant for drug use and abuse as well as previous attempts at rehabilitation. When found, drug paraphernalia, including nitrous oxide canisters were present in the room.

At autopsy, there was no evidence of trauma. There was microscopic evidence of bilateral acute bronchopneumonia, consistent with aspiration.

Toxicological examination of body fluids revealed cocaine at 99 ng/ml, benzoylecgonine at 2000 ng/ml, ecgonine methyl ester at 350 ng/ml, and methadone at 350 ng/ml.

The manner of death is accident.

This is an excerpt from the coroner's report following Chris's death.

Aftermath

Chris had begun using drugs at the age of fourteen and died at twenty-one.

It had been a grueling seven years of loss and of extreme efforts to try to save him from his addiction. Chris went to rehab five times over those years, and we still lost him.

The coroner's report stated that Chris had died of an accidental overdose of cocaine and methadone. Both of those drugs can deprive the brain of oxygen. Both of those drugs can also deprive a father of his son.

The sheriff's office requested to search Chris's room, and I gave them consent to do so. An officer came and went through his things. I wish I could say that he didn't find anything significant, but considering how long Chris had been using, I knew that was unlikely. During their search, the officer found two bongs, rolling papers, an empty whipped cream nitrous canister, a CD case with suspected cocaine, a straw, and razor blades. They found a bowl of marijuana in the bottom of his desk drawer, and a brown bottle with marijuana in it on the floor next to the bed. They also retrieved a bag of marijuana and a marijuana pipe from the pocket in his shorts. These things were the evidence of a killer that took away my son.

The funeral was held at St. Mary's.

There was standing room only, and the array of people who had gathered to say goodbye to Chris was amazing. He had touched many different lives. They ranged from Ms. Tina who had taken care of him in preschool at Westminster Church School, to his basketball teammates from Abbeville, a lady named Miss Josie from his favorite high school, and his math teacher from Tech who whispered to me that Chris was making an "A" in her class. The young man who had given Chris the methadone pills to sell was there at the funeral right alongside family members, friends, classmates, and some of my business associates who were present.

For my part, I was numb. I was not initially even sure that I could make myself go to the funeral. I had been divorced from Mary for about forty-five days by the time of the funeral. I had lost my marriage and I had lost my son. I felt as though I had lost myself. I remember hearing the service but not hearing it. I have a recording of the funeral that I have never listened to.

Shortly after Chris's death, I received an email from a friend of mine named Bob Reuschle. In it he said, "There are few things worse than losing a child." and "This too shall pass though it will never be the same." The first was true. There are few things I can imagine worse than the loss I felt at Chris's death. I am less certain of his words "This too shall pass." It is definitely true that it has never been the same, but the grief is tenacious. There are days when I think about the loss less than other days, but the loss of a son leaves a mark on a father that I am not sure ever fully passes. To quote a popular lyric from Willie Nelson, "It's not something you get over; it's something you get through."

I tried to grieve, but I wasn't entirely sure how. There was no handbook for the loss of a child, and if there had been, I could not have brought myself to read it at the time. I did things that seemed appropriate, making donations in his memory to things that mattered to him, to me, or both. I donated a monetary gift to the school he had loved. I received a letter back thanking me and letting me know that a bookplate bearing his name would be placed in a hymnal or Book of Common Prayer to be used in the worship services in their new chapel. I was looking for some absolution from the pain and for some hope, but I was not yet certain when or if that would come.

In Loving Memory of

Christopher Roberts Grant

May 16, 1984
to
October 17, 2005

23rd Psalm

*The Lord is my shepherd; I shall not want.
He maketh me to lie down in green pastures;
He leadeth me beside the still waters;
He restoreth my soul; He leadeth me in the
paths of righteousness for His name's sake.
Yea though I walk through the valley of
the shadow of death, I will fear no evil;
for Thou art with me; Thy rod and Thy
staff they comfort me. Thou preparest a
table before me in the presence of mine
enemies; Thou anointest my head with oil,
my cup runneth over. Surely goodness and
mercy shall follow me all the days of my
life; and I shall dwell in the House of
the Lord forever.*

Thomas McAfee Funeral Home, Downtown

This is the mass card from Chris's funeral. The words "Yea though I walk through the valley of the shadow of death" had never been more real to me than during this loss.

Sometimes you get discouraged
Because I am so small
And always leave my fingerprints
On furniture and walls.

But every day I'm growing—
I'll be grown up someday
And all those tiny handprints
Will surely fade away.

So here's a final handprint
Just so you can recall
Exactly how my fingers looked
When I was very small.

Christopher Grant
1987

The poem from Chris's handprint photo at three takes on different poignancy when reading it now. "Here's one final handprint Just so you can recall Exactly how my fingers looked When I was very small."

Though substance use damages relationships over time, it does not erase them. There is nothing that Chris could have ever done that would make me un-love him. Likewise, when using he at times acted in ways that seemed unloving. It was not that he loved me any less; it's that there was a chemical barrier between him and his love for me. I still love him, and I miss him every single day.

Patterns

Earlier I shared a bit about the response of my mother after my sister passed away, how she used alcohol as a means of coping with grief. Having seen this firsthand, one might suppose that I learned from the mistakes of my mother. I did not. After Chris died, I found myself drinking more frequently than I had in the past. On the one-year anniversary of Chris's death, I went out with a friend of mine for pizza.

Normally if I were drinking, I would do so in the quiet of my den or on the back deck of the house and then fall asleep in front of the TV. This night while out with my friend, I had a few beers. We returned home without incident, but I was feeling restless and keyed up. Ultimately, I decided to use that nervous energy in a productive way and decided to go in to work for a while. I was pulled over by law enforcement and was asked to blow into the breathalyzer. The ironic thing is that I found myself trying to remember what Chris had always said about when you get pulled over and whether you should blow into the breathalyzer or not. I blew, and I spent the night in jail. My blood alcohol content level had been right on the line of sobriety on the breathalyzer. Unfortunately, it was on the wrong side of the line. Jail is no fun at any time, but late on a Friday night was particularly rough. I was charged with driving under the influence (DUI) and was not released until the early hours of the morning on the following day.

When I was released, I felt relieved. As much as being relieved for being released, I was equally relieved that no one knew, especially no one in my family. In our area, there is a small, local publication where the mugshots of local arrests are printed. Unbeknownst to me, the mother of one of Kelly's friends saw the photo and shared it with her son. Her son shared it with Kelly. In our state, the DUI meant that I kept a yellow stripe on my driver's license over the next six months as I awaited the hearing. I found myself being asked why I had the yellow stripe all the time when I needed to show ID for a check or at the store. When the hearing date finally came almost two years after the charge was received, the officer was not prepared for the hearing. The end result was that the charge was pled down to reckless driving.

During this period, I did not slow down my drinking.

Over the next couple of years, I settled into a pattern of regularly drinking gin, vodka, and scotch. I was taking in about a ½ gallon every three days. When I would finish a bottle, I would place it in a large trash can in my garage in plain sight. Around the three-year anniversary of Chris's death, my mother was visiting me at my home. Upon her arrival that night, she saw the trash can full of bottles in the garage and came to me to ask what that was about. With her one gentle confrontation, I realized that I was well on my way to a problem. I decided to seek some help for myself and called a local treatment facility. I told Kelly and my loved ones that I was checking out for a while and entered residential services that turned out to be a two-week stay. Initially, I went into the program for substance use. Shortly after beginning my treatment, I was moved to the psychiatric unit. Essentially, my therapist felt that I was self-medicating my grief. I would love to have argued with them, but I couldn't. Without intending to, I had repeated the exact same pattern as my mother had followed. Gratefully, my mother, who had been through it before, was able to help me before my using got much worse.

KELLY

Mr. Big Shot

Up until this point, this story has focused primarily on my oldest son, Chris, but I was blessed with two sons. My youngest son, Kelly Frederick Grant, was born in Greenville on May 12, 1986, when Chris was just under two years old.

As is often the case for siblings, Chris and Kelly were night and day with regards to their personalities.

Kelly was the sort of kid who wanted to believe in things like Santa Claus and magic. For those of you who either are or who had an older brother, you know that some beliefs can get disillusioned fairly early in life by the older sibling. Even so, Kelly loved Christmas time. Whatever present he received, he was excited and usually announced that it was "the best thing ever" and that it was exactly what he had wanted! We would often order his gifts online or through catalogs and have them delivered to the house to keep life simple.

As Kelly began to get a little bit older, he still wanted to believe in Santa, but he wasn't sure if the whole Santa Claus thing was real. During one particular Christmas season, as I tucked him in one night after reading him bedtime stories, Kelly looked up at me, narrowed his eyes, and confided to me, conspiratorially in a whisper, "I know who Santa is."

Eating brownies was something we often did in our home when the kids were small. One of the great joys of Kelly's childhood was to eat the "extra" batter in the bowl. This photo is of Kelly at the door and about to get cleaned up after enjoying some delicious batter!

This is the cover page from a biography Kelly wrote about himself that included his birthdate, his family, and some of his future dreams as well!

His future plans are to be a writer. Kelly says that his hero is his dad because he is his parent.

By: Mackensie Yale

One of Kelly's dreams, when he was little, was to be a writer. Here is his rendering of his first book cover for his book on dogs.

I was stunned but recovered quickly, striving my best to keep my poker face intact.

"Who?" I asked, as innocently as I could manage. His voice was a soft whisper, "It's the UPS man!"

Kelly loved to be read to ever since he was a young child. I think I read *Pat the Bunny, The Giving Tree, The Little Mouse, The Ripe Red Strawberry,* and *The Big Hungry Bear* over 1,000 times to both Kelly and Chris over the years. He loved to sing along with a cassette tape at the top of his lungs from the back seat of the car. Raffi was his favorite, and he sang "The More We Get Together" with gusto!

In July of 1996, Kelly was ten years old and attended Gwynn Valley Camp for younger boys in Brevard, NC. A note from one of the workers there referenced Kelly's shyness, being a team player, knowing when to be quiet and when to listen, and described him as a polite young man. I would say that they had a pretty good assessment of him. He was a bit more reserved than some other boys his age, but he was definitely a team player. He was polite and was probably a more adept student than Chris had been. As I said, Chris and Kelly were very different children.

Whereas Kelly loved to be read to and later to read himself, I am not sure Chris ever read an entire book even when doing book reports on them in school.

Also, though Chris and Kelly were both gifted kids, Kelly's gifts leaned more towards music than athletics. Even so, Kelly had a desire to make his dad proud, and he knew I loved sports. In all honesty, he was not naturally athletic, but he consistently showed up, and he tried hard. What he lacked in raw talent, he made up for in heart and hustle. All through their childhood, I coached both of the kids in sports. Since they were attending a private, faith-based school at the time, it meant that the rules about the sports teams were a little bit different. One major difference was that every student on the team was required to have some time playing during each half of every game. I had been coaching Kelly in basketball for around seven years, and in all of those years, he had never scored even one single point in a game— not a single one. I knew it, he knew it, the parents of all of the players knew it, and everybody who came to the games knew it.

Throughout these years Kelly had developed an unofficial pre-game ritual of shooting basketball in the driveway on game days before it was time to leave for the game. On one particular Saturday morning, as we got into the car to head to the game, Kelly looked at me matter-of-factly and said, "I'm going to make a basket today."

From your lips to God's ears, I thought.

The game was underway! We were nearing the end of the season, and this was a big game. As the game continued, we were not playing our best at all. Our star player was having an unusual off game, and the rest of the team seemed to be struggling to keep up as well. Since it was required, Kelly was on the floor playing for his portion of the game. During the game, Kelly got the ball. I expected him to pass the ball as he often did, but instead, he began to drive down the court. He was in the three-point range when he stopped in place and started to take a shot. We emphasized a good passing game, and everybody on our side of the gym knew Kelly had not made a shot his whole life. As he started up, I thought, No! Then I remembered that I was the coach! I opened my mouth to scream NO, but it was too late. The shot was already in the air. Time slowed down as the ball rotated gracefully through the air and drilled right through the center of the rim for three points!

My no turned into a *YES*!!!

Kelly acted like that happened every night, but I almost came out of my shoes! That one shot shifted the momentum of the entire game. Our star player re-grouped, and the rest of the team rallied for the win. Although he was never a star athlete, he was a star in that moment, and he began scoring fairly regularly after that game as well. After that night, the assistant coach started calling Kelly "Mr. Big Shot." It stuck. Everybody started calling him that, and he beamed.

Dear Dad,

You've have always been a great dad and role model. I am very greatful to you for helping me grow and develop over the years. LOVE YA MAN!

Sincerely,

Kelly

Like many parents, I cherish notes and reminders from both of my sons. It means a lot to me that Kelly thought I was a great dad!

The Teen Years

Kelly was active in both church league basketball for St. Mary's and club soccer for the Downtown Soccer Association. He was a good student and had done well academically throughout his early years. By his early teens, Kelly was already struggling with living in the shadow cast by Chris's drug use. At one point after Kelly had gotten into some trouble at school, he was afraid that some of the families in the school wouldn't let their sons hang out with him anymore. Kelly wrote a letter to reach out to his friend's parents in order to try to maintain his friendship with their son. In the letter, he explained he had been suspended at school for doing "a very stupid thing," which he said he regretted and assured them that it wouldn't happen again. In the letter, he specifically stated that he did not use, sell, or come in contact with any controlled substances or illegal drugs. He referenced

Chris having struggled with drugs for four years and being at a rehab in Mississippi at the time, and he clarified that Mary and I had never let Chris keep drugs around the house. He closed the letter by saying he wanted to remain friends with their son and that he had made a "stupid mistake" and with a plea to allow him and their son to remain friends. I kept the letter. I am still struck by Kelly's desire to defend Mary and I and to distinguish himself from his brother's use.

Although he did not write it in the letter, Kelly chose never to visit Chris in rehab. I don't know if he hated seeing him there or if it was for other reasons, but I know that even on the rare family days when Chris was in treatment, Kelly opted not to go. Later on, I learned of an occasion when Chris sold drugs to one of Kelly's best friends. I found out when law enforcement explained to me that Chris had suggested to Kelly's friend that he pawn some of his mother's jewelry to pay him for drugs. Kelly's friend did, and the theft was discovered. The only thing that "saved" Chris on that occasion was the parents did not want to press charges on their son. Law enforcement followed up with the local pawn shop and was able to recover the jewelry. The shadow of Chris's use extended into Kelly's world.

In retrospect, the impact of Chris's use on Kelly was becoming clearer even then. Even so, it can be difficult to separate "normal teenage struggles" from the difficulties that are impacted or exacerbated by substance use within the family.

Throughout his teen years, Kelly did many of the normal things that kids that age often do. He read the entire Goosebumps and Harry Potter series up to that point and loved to read mysteries. His voice cracked frequently. He worked at a pizza place from 2002-2003 and at a fast-food restaurant after that. In the fall of that same year, he applied for "early decision" at Furman University for the class of 2005.

Mary and I had separated in 2003 and legally separated in January of 2004 prior to our divorce in 2005. Most people would remember the day their wife said they wanted to leave them. I have no recollection of that conversation ever happening. I was so immersed in Chris's problems and how to help him that nothing else mattered, even my relationship with my wife. I remember telling my mother that I was getting divorced. I can picture where I was and recall the conversation. We were walking on Sullivan's Island, we stopped, and I said, "Hey Mom, let's sit down on this piece of driftwood. I have to tell you something." I told her I was getting a divorce. She said, "Oh, you've got a girlfriend." I told her the last thing I'd have is a girlfriend; you raised me better than that. I said, "Mary just wants out."

Throughout this time, Chris stayed with me, and Kelly stayed with Mary. Kelly had an innocence but was mature in many ways. He was sheltered at St. Mary's School. Mary gravitated towards Kelly, and I gravitated towards Chris because of sports and because he needed more help once he started using. Kelly was compliant, almost to the end. I remember telling Mary during his time, "You take care of Kelly and I will take care of Christopher." Looking back, that was foolishness, but we were doing the best we knew how to at the time. They were both our sons, and Mary and I loved both of them. The cracks of separation and divorce have a way of spreading throughout the family. As I was increasingly focusing my attention on Chris, Kelly remained with his mother.

In general, Kelly was more driven than Chris had ever seemed to be. Like with his early basketball days, Kelly worked hard in everything he did. While Chris was struggling in his addiction and was in and out of rehabs, Kelly graduated from St. Joseph's Catholic School in the spring of 2004. Although Kelly had applied for early decision with Furman, he ultimately chose not to go there. He considered College of Charleston, but he felt that the environment on campus wouldn't be the best for him at that time. Instead, he decided to enroll at Birmingham Southern and started in the fall of that year.

Kelly was attending school there when Chris died in October of 2005.

A Change of Scenery

One thing I don't think I entirely understood at the time is how close Chris and Kelly had been and how much Chris's death impacted Kelly. In many ways, siblings are often each other's first friends, and that was true of the two of them as well. They had played ball and video games together growing up, and they loved one another. Even when Chris was struggling in his addiction, he had at times tried to encourage Kelly not to go down the path he had, but it's hard for a drowning man to teach someone else to swim. I later learned that Chris and Kelly had used alcohol and marijuana together.

At one point in 2004, Chris and Kelly were arrested together while visiting friends in Charlotte. Chris had been drinking in the car and threw a beer can out of the car window. Since Kelly was driving, he was charged with having an open container in the vehicle. I found out about the charges because, as is still the case today, when someone gets a legal charge, they tend to get inundated with letters from attorneys who are all too eager to "help." The barrage of letters let me know that something was amiss, and, with a little investigation the charges were easy to discover. It would be easy in light of Chris's using first to see Chris as having been the problem. None of this is to say that Kelly did not have some struggles along the way as well that should have been red flags. At that time of the open container charge, Kelly was already attending alcohol and drug abuse classes related to his having gotten a previous DUI. He had spent the night in jail from that charge before a friend of his posted bail for him. Both of my boys were struggling, and then Chris died.

Since Kelly was in school at Birmingham Southern from 2004-2006, he was out of state when Chris died. I wasn't sure how to best let him know; so, I called the school and had a counselor there at the school tell Kelly about Chris's death so he wouldn't be alone when he found out. Kelly drove himself home from Birmingham Southern for the funeral.

Following the funeral, I decided that we were going to get back on the horse quickly. I would miss little work, and Kelly would return to Birmingham Southern to finish the semester. In retrospect, I should have asked Kelly if he wanted to stay home for the remainder of the semester to mourn the death of his brother.

Of course, education was important to me and had always been a strength for Kelly; so, at the start of the next semester, I again encouraged him to return to school. I regret having sent him back to school so soon. He returned to Birmingham, but it was not the same for him and was ultimately short-lived. Kelly decided that he wanted to leave Birmingham Southern and enroll in College of Charleston to be closer to home.

As I mentioned, Kelly was always a good student, and I have kept and read many of his essays from his school years. Looking back and reading through them now, I can see some of the impact of losing Chris had on him. One of the papers he wrote in August of 2006 said, "…the world is far from a perfect place. Death is a very large part of our world." In this same paper, he referenced the divorce which occurred while he was in high school, and his subsequently growing up "faster than other teenagers" that were his friends.

Around that same time, he wrote a paper about Jack London's story, *To Build a Fire*. Some of the excerpts of things he wrote seem poignant in retrospect:

"All this man has to contest nature is his frail human body." "It was as though he had just heard his own sentence of death." (London, 138) "Finally, the man sees the futility of his actions and decides to await death calmly. His impending death brings clarity to the man in his last few moments on earth." "Then the man drowsed off into what seemed to him to be the most comfortable and satisfying sleep he had ever known." (London, 142) "No matter what this man does, death is only a few paces behind him."

I think it is fair to say that Kelly's themes leaned darker than usual during those days. Despite everything, he had some pretty amazing positives going for him as well. For one, he and I loved one another. Even with the struggles we faced, there were beautiful moments and times together along the way. In June of 2006, Kelly gave me a Father's Day Card that called me the "Greatest of All," which I still cherish. Kelly was finding his niche.

This is a birthday card Kelly sent me in April of 2010.

Marching to His Own Beat

I previously mentioned that Kelly was musically inclined, but I could not have guessed in his early years of singing along with the radio just how musically inclined he was. His musicality began to shine through in his playing drums. He had started playing them in high school, but somewhere along the way, his skills in this department seemed to take a huge leap forward when I wasn't looking.

While in Charleston, Kelly met up with an old friend from grade school and they decided to start a band together. They were actually pretty good and began to play some locally. Word of them spread pretty quickly, and it did not take long before they began touring across all of North America. Things were looking up for my son's musical pursuits, and it was great to see him passionate about something again. Since I was not at the height of coolness in the college music scene, it took me a little longer than you might expect before I finally got the opportunity to hear them play live myself during a concert at the Music Farm in Charleston. As I stood there and watched Kelly play, I thought, who is this kid? It seemed like he had gone from playing around on the drums to becoming an incredible drummer overnight.

The band continued to tour and play across the country and in Canada, even playing at South by Southwest in Austin, Texas. Admittedly, I am Kelly's father; so, it might be easy to dismiss my words about Kelly's musicianship as a father's pride. I wasn't the only one who noticed his talent.

Following the Austin show, a local paper reviewed the band and in his write up the reviewer said that although he was not sure where the band was headed, the drummer was "definitely going places." Although I was extremely supportive of his music, fame can be a fickle friend, and I encouraged him to remain focused on finishing school.

Unbeknownst to me even as Kelly's musical career was progressing, so too was his substance use.

Shortly after Kelly returned from the North American tour, I received a bill at home from an emergency room in Charleston. A few things threw me about that. First of all, I had no idea that Kelly had gone to an emergency room or why. Second, Kelly had not used his insurance card. I called him up to find out what had happened. During the call, Kelly explained that the band had just finished up a hard three-and-a-half-day drive coming back from a show, everyone was exhausted, and that it was extremely hot. He said that when they got back and were unloading the equipment, he passed out in the parking lot and his friends took him to the emergency room. I asked him why he had not used his insurance card. He said that since his friends had taken him to the emergency room, he didn't have his wallet with him. It seemed plausible; so, I paid the bill and honestly didn't think much more about it.

About a month later, during his junior year, I got a call from a friend of Kelly's who asked me if I remembered the time that Kelly passed out and had gone to the ER. I confirmed that I did remember. What he said next shook me to my core. He told me that Kelly hadn't passed out; he had overdosed on heroin.

My heart sank.

I kept thinking this can't be happening again.

By this time, I knew that Kelly drank some and smoked marijuana occasionally. Almost everyone thought that was the extent of things. Kelly kept his opiate use hidden.

I mentioned earlier having neglected Kelly due to being preoccupied with Chris's growing addiction. Having a family member who struggles with addiction can be all-consuming, and my relationship with Kelly was part of what was consumed. In retrospect, even after Chris's death, I missed some telling signs related to Kelly's growing substance use. The storm clouds had been gathering; but somehow, I had not heard the thunder. I had already mentioned Kelly's first DUI and his subsequent open-container violation with Chris. In January of 2007, Kelly received another DUI in Greenville, SC. At the advice of his attorney, he requested a jury trial, and ultimately the charge was pled down to reckless driving and Kelly paid a fine of a few hundred dollars. In September of 2010, Kelly received an additional DUI and a simple possession of marijuana charge. This call was the crack of thunder that helped me to see the clouds that had been quietly gathering.

As soon as I heard that Kelly's passing out had been an overdose, I immediately got in my car and drove to Charleston to bring Kelly home. I would love to tell you that I had a great plan for when I got him, but I had no idea what I was going to say or do. I had tunnel vision; all I could see or think of was getting to my son. My head was spinning, and I was clearly not firing on all cylinders during the drive. At one point, I went through a drive-through at a fast-food restaurant in Clinton, SC, paid at the first window, and then pulled off from the restaurant. I was more than two miles down the road before I realized I didn't stop at the second window to pick up my food. All I could think about was getting to my son. Kelly was in trouble, and I needed to know that he was ok.

At this point in 2010, I had not heard anything about anyone using heroin. There was no opioid epidemic in the headlines then. I did know that Kelly wore long-sleeve shirts all the time, but I had chalked it up to adolescent weirdness and the "younger generation" fashions. I didn't know that wearing long sleeves is common to cover needle marks on the arms. When I finally got to Charleston, I talked to Kelly. I talked *at* him might be a more accurate description, at least initially. I told him that he was coming back home with me, and shortly after that, we got in the car to drive the three and a half hours back home. He was beyond angry. During those three and a half hours, he called me every name in the book. He poured out all of his hurt over Chris, our family, the separation, and the divorce. Once again, I tried to give him the space to vent his feelings and hopefully to find some healing in doing so. He said that I should never have forced him to go back to school following Chris's death before he was ready. Unsure of what else to say, I was mostly quiet and let him vent, hoping that getting things off of his chest might help draw off some of the poisonous anger that seemed to have seeped in through his hurt.

When we got back home, Kelly lived with me and he saw a counselor. He had gotten a psychiatrist in Charleston after his initial "pass out." I drug tested Kelly every other day over the summer to help ensure that he was not using. He was struggling, but he seemed to be doing ok. He even took a summer class at a local technical college.

In August, Kelly returned to Charleston and the band. I had spoken with the band members, and we had an agreement. If Kelly used, they agreed to let me know, and I would send him to rehabilitation. This way, the band could stay intact, and (since Kelly was legally an adult) I could offer him some accountability and had some "leverage" to help encourage him to stay on track. Since I was financially contributing to the band's travels and his bandmates cared about him, they agreed. The band itself was continuing to do well and signed a recording contract with a well-known record label. Things were looking up, and the sky was the limit. It seemed like Kelly and the band were on the verge of making it big!

Then Kelly used.

Though I was scared for my son, it seemed like our plan was going as we had agreed. The band members let me know that Kelly had used again. I was ready to implement the plan to send Kelly to a rehab facility in North Carolina. But the band took a different course, and I no longer had "leverage to get him to go to rehab." In October of 2010, they decided to move on without Kelly.

Kelly was devastated. I was too. Without the incentive of returning to the band, Kelly decided not to go into treatment and came back home.

I later learned, ironically, that it was a member of the band who had introduced Kelly to heroin.

Struggles

Part of this story is how different the experience was with Kelly compared to Chris. In some ways they were close. After all the rehabs, Chris moved out. He decided that he was going to live on his own in a hotel on Mauldin Road. He had Kelly, convinced that he would live with him, but I was not going to let that happen. He wanted to try to drag Kelly down with him. A lot of what we did was to protect Kelly. That was probably why I sent Chris to Abbeville and why we decided to split the boys up when Mary and I separated.

Before Chris's funeral, I looked out the front door window and there he was smoking a cigarette with his friends. I was stunned. I thought Kelly never smoked a cigarette in his life. I turned and thought, okay, big boy. With Kelly, it was so different.

In March of 2010, Kelly was a senior in college. He was studying psychology, had a desire to help others, and was a member of a band that had recently signed a record deal. In some ways, he seemed to be doing pretty well. He was vulnerable from the loss of his brother and the divorce of his parents. It was around this time that his bandmate and friend introduced him to heroin, presumably to help him through a tough time.

When I learned that Kelly had used again in October of 2010, we talked about it. With the band broken up, we both knew he was struggling. Ultimately, we decided that he would come back home from school and would stay with me. Kelly told me he could quit on his own. Having tried the rehab route with Chris, I was more open to trying something different in an effort to help Kelly. When Kelly came home for those two months in October before his death, I drug tested him several times a week. When we got his results, there was always THC in his screen. I was looking for heroin or any kind of opioid. He always tested negative for those. I later learned that heroin goes through your system quickly and is usually not detected unless the test is given often.

Kelly was working and had rented a small house in town not far from where I lived. He was trying to avoid the attraction of heroin. In November of 2010, unbeknownst to me, Kelly had contacted his supplier in Charleston and ordered some drugs through the mail via a MoneyGram. I have the receipt from the order with the amount of $110.00. The total was $121.00 with fees. The package was delivered, but he did not immediately use it. Kelly was actively fighting his illness and was trying not to use.

On December 5, 2010, we were getting ready to head into the holidays. There was a pair of shoes that I knew Kelly wanted, and I had decided to surprise him with them for Christmas while I was out shopping. The problem was that I wasn't sure what size shoe Kelly wore. I called to get his shoe size to be sure they would fit, but I couldn't get him. Kelly usually always answered when I called or else would call me back a few minutes after I left a message.

Rather than wait and have to fight traffic again, I bought the shoes, figuring that if worse came to worst I could bring them back. As the day went on, Kelly had still not returned my call, which was not like him. Even so, I figured that I would see him later that evening when we got together for our new routine of watching Mad Men together on Sunday nights. When Kelly did not show up for the show, my anxiety went up, and I began to get a now familiar sinking feeling in my stomach.

I called Kelly again and still got no answer. I decided that I would go by the rental house to check on him. When I arrived at his apartment, his car was there; I got out and rang the bell. No one answered, and my anxiety level was exploding. My heart was racing, and something close to panic began to well up in me. I knocked at the door and again there was no answer. I looked through the window into the house and could see that the door was locked from the inside. He had to be inside. Not knowing what else to do but knowing that I had to know Kelly was ok, I picked up a brick, broke the small window on the door, and reached through the broken glass to open it. I walked in with my heart racing and my anxiety going through the roof, calling out to him as I went.

I turned the corner to his room. I found Kelly curled up in a fetal position with a rubber band around his bicep and a needle in his arm. He was wearing Furman basketball shorts and tie-dyed t-shirt he loved. In a sense, Chris had died prettier than Kelly. He was already lying on his floor and appeared to have fallen asleep. That was not the case for Kelly. He had clearly fallen to the floor and had vomited. All I did for the next fifteen minutes was sit down on the floor next to Kelly and cry into my hands. Then, for the second time in my life, I called 911 to report the death of a son. Words cannot adequately convey how surreal it was to watch a second body bag being taken to the back of a truck, knowing that my son's lifeless body was inside.

On the opposite side of the room was his cell phone, full of missed calls from me. In one sense, that sums up some of what it is to lose a child. There are unanswered calls. There is an unfulfilled lease. There are unworn shoes. There are uncompleted degrees. There is an unlived life. There are grandchildren that I will never hold and an entire world of unfulfilled dreams. Yes, addiction is a thief; it steals a person's future from them, and from those who love them. In this moment, the theft was so tremendous that I felt I had nothing left.

I knew that Kelly was gone, and I still called 911 for EMS. According to the coroner's report and death certificate, Kelly died at approximately 2:00 am on December 5, 2010, of "Accidental Acute Morphine Toxicity." He had used heroin for only about nine months in total and was only twenty-four years old. Per the coroner's report, Kelly had only two needle marks on his body, evidence of how hard he was working to quit using. On the day that he died, one of the last phone calls he made was to his longtime friend, Anna. He asked her if she knew where he could get some Suboxone because he was feeling a little "jonesy." Anna told him that she didn't know what Suboxone was. Even his long-term friends like Anna didn't have any idea of his heroin addiction. I wish he would have asked me that day if I knew where he could get some Suboxone. By this time, I knew what it was and would have understood why he wanted it.

The day after Kelly died, I went back over to the place he was renting in Greenville to start cleaning out his stuff. The neighbor from across the street saw me there. She waved to me, and I waved back to her. I didn't know her. Kelly had only lived there a short period of time. She walked towards me, and I walked towards her home to meet her. She seemed to be a nice older woman. She told me that she had brought cookies over to Kelly when he moved in and what a nice young man he was. She said she realized he had died yesterday. She wanted me to know that he was very polite and that he had come back to thank her again for the cookies, which made her feel good.

Sometimes we think of these kids as different, but they are not, they are just normal kids.

Within a few days, I found myself at the funeral of my last living child. He was stolen from me by the same thief who took my first son, an insidious thief who dared to return to the scene of the crime. I do not mean the exact same chemical, of course; I mean the exact same disease. Addiction had taken both of my sons, and the scene of the crime was the hearts of all of those who loved them.

Mary requested that Kelly's funeral be held at the church she had attended since our divorce, St. Anthony's. The facility itself was smaller, and the sanctuary was full to capacity with people–people who loved Kelly and knew him from childhood and people who had gone to school with him. Kids I didn't know from Birmingham

Southern, and kids who had played music with him made the trip to attend. Also present were those who love Mary and me. Although their presence means a great deal to me now, at the time, I simply felt empty…almost as if I were detached from the world. As we moved to the graveside portion of the service, a family member requested that the coffin be opened. She placed a cross inside before they closed the lid the final time, closing in my baby boy.

The grief was a scalding, eviscerating thing; honestly, at that time, I had no idea how I would get through it. The rituals of mourning are much easier to navigate than the labyrinth of grief. I have healed a great deal since that time, but some days, I am still looking for my way out. Loss is an event; grief is a process.

Probate court later estimated Kelly's personal estate to have a value of $0. I have his wallet from the day he died. It has exactly the same things in it that it had then—his driver's license, a bank card, an alumni card from both his high school and college, and one dollar. His estimated net worth was zero. Never confuse net worth with personal worth. His worth to me was immeasurable.

One night soon after Kelly died, I was watching TV. There was a segment about a couple who were taking care of a foster child. He was a good football player. The couples house had just burned down, and they lost everything in the fire. The media provided a phone number to contact them if you could help. I called the number and explained that my son had passed away. I asked for the young man's size and was told that he was 6 foot and 170 pounds with a size 11 shoe. I said, "Wow, that is amazing. Kelly had all kinds of good clothing, boots, and shoes." They came over the next day, and everything fit. Kelly was smaller than Chris for the longest time. In the end, he was taller than his brother. He was just a late bloomer in terms of height.

CONSENT TO SEARCH

Case #: _2-10-101337_

Date: _01/04/11_

Time: _09.39_

I, _STEPHEN M. GRANT_, having been informed of my constitutional right not to have a search made of the premises listed below without a search warrant, do authorize

D.P. GARRISON and _R.L. FLOYD_ Police Officers of the City of Greenville, South Carolina, to conduct a complete search of the premises indicated below. This consent is given voluntarily and I understand that I have the right to refuse and that I can withdraw at any time. I also understand that anything found can be used against me. There have been no threats or promises made to me.

Following Kelly's death, I gave law enforcement permission to search the premises. I am not sure what I thought they might find. I knew the list of things that were found in Chris's room, and perhaps I wanted to be sure that Kelly had not been using in the same way. Perhaps I hoped that they would find me there. At this point I certainly felt lost.

Toxicology Report

Report Issued 12/10/2010 09:01

To: 10269
Greenville County Medical Examiner
Attn: Dr. Micheal Ward
690 W. Faris, Ste. 110
Greenville, SC 29605

Patient Name	GRANT, KELLY
Patient ID	A10-476
Chain	11231664
Age	24 Y
Gender	Male
Workorder	10269690
Page 1 of 4	

Positive Findings:

Compound	Result	Units	Matrix Source
Delta-9 THC	1.8	ng/mL	Femoral Blood
Delta-9 Carboxy THC	20	ng/mL	Femoral Blood
Codeine - Free	18	ng/mL	Femoral Blood
Morphine - Free	210	ng/mL	Femoral Blood

See Detailed Findings section for additional information

Testing Requested:

Analysis Code	Description
60518	Postmortem Toxicology - Basic, Blood

This is the toxicology report for Kelly following his death. All too often the "cause of death" reads "accident" rather than listing the actual substances that led to the death of yet another human being–a person whose light the world needed.

VICTIM'S NAME: GRANT, KELLY FREDRICK

BYPRODUCT OF HEROIN. WHEN HEROIN IS USED, IT IS VERY CONVERTED TO MORPHINE, AND OFTEN TIMES THE ONLY T EVIDENCE OF HEROIN ABUSE IS THE PRESENCE OF A FATAL MORPHINE.

THE CAUSE OF DEATH IN THIS CASE IS ACUTE MORPHINE TOXICITY.

CONTRIBUTING FACTOR INCLUDES BACTERIAL MYOCARDI

THE MANNER OF DEATH IS ACCIDENT.

Kelly Frederick Grant

Born in Greenville, SC on May 12, 1986 Departed on Dec. 5, 2010 and resided in Greenville, SC.

Visitation: Tuesday, Dec. 7, 2010

Service: Wednesday, Dec. 8, 2010

Cemetery: Woodlawn Memorial Park

Please click on the links above for locations, times, maps, and directions.

Kelly Frederick Grant

[SIGN GUESTBOOK]   [VIEW GUESTBOOK]

Kelly Frederick Grant, 24, died Sunday, December 5, 2010.
Born in Greenville, he was the son of Mary McGoldrick and Stephen Michael Grant.
Kelly was a senior at the College of Charleston and a member of St. Anthony of Padua Catholic Church.
He loved animals, especially dogs, and loved music. He was a drummer in the band Co.
Surviving, in addition to his parents, are grandparents, John and Margaret McGoldrick of Brevard, NC and Louis and Dorothy Grant of Abbeville, SC. He was predeceased by a brother, Christopher Roberts Grant.
In lieu of flowers, memorials may be made to St. Anthony of Padua Catholic School Building Fund, 307 Gower St., Greenville, SC 29611 or St. Joseph's Catholic School, 100 St. Joseph's St., Greenville, SC 29607 or the Humane Society of Greenville County 328 Furman Hall Rd., Greenville, SC 29609.
Visitation will be Tuesday, December 7, 2010 from 6 to 7:30 p.m. at Thomas McAfee Funeral Home, Downtown. The funeral Mass will be

This is Kelly's obituary–the hopes and dreams of a lifetime, condensed to just over 150 words.

Every Loss is Different

With Chris, I had a chance to mourn before he ever died in some ways. I had mourned every time he did not come home on time. I had mourned when he was away at rehab. I had mourned when he was in jail. I had mourned when he had a recurrence. Chris seemed wired to seek a pharmaceutical answer to everything. On the nights I'd sit up and worry about him, I had played through countless frightening scenarios. I had lost him a thousand times before I ever lost him. For those reasons, his death was no less of a blow; it was a blow I had an opportunity to brace myself for. I had worked through some of my anticipatory grief.

With Kelly, I did not have that same opportunity. The blow caught me off guard, and I did not have the time to consider losing him in the same way.

When you lose someone you love, you can't compare one loss to another adequately.

Does it hurt worse to lose one's mother or to lose one's child?

Does it hurt worse to lose a brother or to lose a best friend?

Every loss is different.   Every loss is unique.   Every loss hurts.

Experiencing loss and grief takes an emotional toll on a person.

Love costs us something.

Who knows the real cost of addiction?

I don't mean financial costs. There are degrees that will never be earned. There are transcripts that are unfinished and will never be finished. There are unwritten songs and broken up bands. There are unlived lives and silenced dreams. There are parentless children and childless parents. There is a deep chasm of loss named addiction, and it cannot be filled...not even by every life that has fallen into it from the beginning. It can only be spanned.

HOPE

Remembering

It was October 16, 2011, almost exactly six years since Chris's death and a year since Kelly's. In the interceding years, my mother had gotten sick with cancer and moved in with me so that I could assist with her caretaking. She was scheduled to get her final PET scan the following day to see if the treatment had worked.

I am a bit of a packrat when it comes to my family. I still had lots of unorganized items lying around. I found a stack of photos of my parents when they were about 30 years old that I thought Mom might like to see. I put them in a folder for her along with a picture of Chris. As she was sorting through the photos, she commented on some then paused before handing me the one of Chris. As she held it out, she asked when it was taken and if I had seen it. I responded that of course, I had seen the picture before but that I couldn't say exactly how long it had been. It was a photo of Chris playing soccer when he was around fifteen years old. It was not the picture that she meant. She said, "You better sit down because you have to see what is written on the back."

I sat down on the edge of the bed as she turned over the photo. On the back were three words written in Chris's messy, beautiful handwriting:

Don't forget me

I had not, not even for a second. I still have not.

At times the pain of grief was overwhelming, and at times, I would laugh at some memory that came to mind of things that my boys had said and done. If I had lost one son, it would have been an epidemic in my own life. The loss of Chris touched everything and changed how I saw the world. To lose Kelly as well felt as though the epidemic had become extinction. I felt hollow, and as though I had died inside myself.

This is not a story of statistics and epidemics. This is a story about being a parent, about loving someone struggling with substance use, and about loss on a scale that few can imagine. It is also a story about what comes next.

Don't forget me

I had not, not even for a second.
I still have not.

SOME THINGS I LEARNED AND EXPERIENCED ALONG THE WAY

Next

After the shock of losing my sons began to give way to grief in earnest, I wondered how I could continue on. I used to be known as the insurance guy, or the baseball coach at St. Joseph's, now I am known as the guy who lost both of his sons to drug overdoses.

When I was in the worst of my grief, I ached and hurt so deeply that I felt there would never be anything except sadness. When I was in this time of tremendous suffering, it was like being in an ocean, with no land in sight. I was swimming, but I had no direction, no goal. I was trying not to go under, and that effort took everything I had. I was tired, weary beyond imagination, but I was still swimming.

Eventually, in the midst of trying to stay afloat, I remembered that there was such a thing as life, and that it was time to go to shore. I remembered the shore, but that didn't mean that I could see it. I was on top of the water, most days, but I began to believe that maybe there was some greater purpose in my pain and their loss; if there was no purpose now, maybe there could be later. At the time, I could not have articulated that, but in looking back, I can see the beginnings of hope there. I could not see the shore, but even hope this fragile was a life preserver. I did not know which way the shore was. My grief had no direction. It was a vast ocean, and I was still lost.

My first real glimpse of a shoreline came in a way I never expected. It came through my work at a business retreat called a "boot camp" in January of 2011. I was not excited about it. It was a sales retreat, and sales was my background. I was grieving. I wanted to be a team player and set a good example; reluctantly, I went. In that sense, I suppose I gave the speakers the gift of low expectations!

Two guys from St. Louis, John O'Leary and Ben Newman, facilitated the boot camp. John was a burn survivor who had recovered from burns over the majority of his body when he was a young boy, and Ben was a successful Northwestern Mutual Representative. Both have gone on to become nationally and internationally known motivational speakers and have published successful books telling their stories as well. At the time, I knew that I wasn't excited to be attending. Once the meeting started, I was surprised to hear them say that they were not there to spend three days helping us become a better salesperson. They said they were there to help us crystalize what our legacy was going to be when we left this world. I began to get a little more interested and leaned in to pay closer attention. I had never considered that question before, and I certainly didn't think I had an answer for what my legacy would be at that moment. Nevertheless, they went around the room and asked each of us to stand and tell them what we thought our legacy would be. When it was my turn, I opened my mouth without any hesitation and said, "I want my legacy to be that I did everything I could to help adolescents and young adults who struggle with addiction, substance use, and mental illness."

What was amazing about that statement was it was the furthest thing from my mind. Kelly had passed just weeks before, and quite frankly, although it's my nature to be compassionate, the last thing on my mind was to help others. I recall that moment often. I believe that God gave me the words to say that day.

At that moment, I drew a line in the sand and jumped off the pier into the dark, not knowing if there was any water.

On that day, although I did not know what it would become or exactly what it would look like at the time, Chris and Kelly's HOPE began to form.

Shortly after the three-day event, I met with a friend and he encouraged me to reach out to Bob Morris at the Community Foundation of Greenville. I scheduled time to meet with Bob and presented him with the idea of Chris and Kelly's HOPE Foundation. By the end of our conversation, he gave me his blessing to move forward and even waived the fee to start since they didn't have anything in their donor advised funds that dealt with adolescent and young adult addiction. If it had not been for the Community Foundation and Mr. Morris's staff, Chris and Kelly's HOPE might not have gotten off the ground.

Someone asked me a while back what the "HOPE" was to me in Chris and Kelly's HOPE. Following such a loss, what hope could there be? There are three primary answers to that question.

One answer is that I want to do everything in my power to connect people struggling with addiction and other substance use disorders to the help they need. In that capacity, I began trying to educate myself about resources in the community and telling others about them. Through Chris and Kelly's HOPE, we have helped refer countless individuals to providers in their communities, supported non-profits whose purpose is to treat addictions, and at times have even been able to help with expenses for their treatment. There are blue signs to direct people to hospitals when they have an immediate medical need, but there are no blue signs for treatment from substance use disorders. The more we can raise awareness of the resources available for recovery, the greater the possibility for those who are struggling to find those resources. I hope we will help countless more as they begin their recovery.

A second answer and source of hope is my faith. After Chris's accident, mentioned earlier in the book, I told him that God must be looking out for him. Neither my faith nor the faith of my family has been perfect throughout the years. That said, it is my faith that has made my heartache bearable. I find comfort in the hope that I will be with my sons again in the future.

My third and final answer relates to my hope for Chris and Kelly's HOPE Foundation. I want everyone to understand that they are not alone.

If you have a loved one struggling with substance use, you are not alone.

If you are sitting up at night worrying about a loved one, you are not alone.

If you have a loved one who you barely recognize anymore because of the impact of the drugs on their life, you are not alone.

If you live in constant fear that you will get the call telling you that your loved one is gone, you are not alone.

If you have received the call telling you that they are gone, you are still not alone.

If you are grieving and feel depressed, or anxious, or empty, you are not alone.

This acknowledgment that we are not alone is an important lesson that I have learned along the way.

We Need Each Other

Concerning substance use disorders, we have a word for people who are in recovery by themselves; we call it "high."

The author John Dunne had it right, "No man is an island unto himself," and there is no such thing as recovery in isolation. Addiction is a vicious disease, and one of its most vicious aspects is the way that it robs a person of the things that are most important to them. Left unchecked and over time, addiction will take away one's time, health, resources, freedom, and even their lives. It will also steal one's relationships.

The person suffering from addiction used to have a bad day and call up a family member or friend, now they call their dealer or friends who use.

The person in active use may have stopped by their mom's in the past when they faced a difficult decision, but now they stop by the bar.

In the beginning, the drug seems to promise connections with other people— invitations to parties, good times with friends, and feeling more socially at ease for some, and temporarily it seems to deliver. It is always temporary.

Drugs are a jealous lover, and they will not abide any other relationships in the lives of those who are addicted. Physiologically, alcohol and other drugs literally dysregulate the part of the brain designed to help us connect with others. Eventually, the drug won't leave any room in a person's life for those relationships. The parent who does not use drugs is not morally superior to the one who is using. The parent who is using has a chemical barrier between them and those they love. It is not a matter of feelings of affection or a desire to be a good parent; it is a chemical barrier that cuts us off from our ability to connect with others. That same chemical barrier exists for all relationships. To be in a healthy relationship, we have to be both capable of being and willing to be vulnerable enough to be who we really are, to risk being loved. We cannot be who we are while being a chemically augmented version of ourselves. To be in active addiction is to experience a profound sense of isolation.

In recovery, we regain our ability to connect with other human beings without the use of substances. We are literally physiologically created for connection. Our limbic systems, mirror neurons, and ability to learn socially are all wired to help us connect. That system is the heart of what is damaged in substance use disorders. As we begin to heal, we must do so in a social environment. We need other people in our lives. We need other recovering people in our lives as well, not just for the advice and wisdom that they can share but also because of their profound empathy. Their understanding can provide a profound sense of belonging. Their presence can offer a stable limbic system that we can attune to, which helps us better regulate our own limbic system.

This is also true of grief. There may be times when you do need some time to yourself, but recovery from grief does not happen in isolation. If I had not gone to the business retreat, I may have never begun to understand what I wanted my legacy to be. As I have shared my story in recent years, I have had countless others come up to me and share their pain with me as well. My vulnerability about my loss opens the doorway for a healing connection.

Some days I swim in the grief of losing Chris and Kelly. A giant wave of grief and loss crashes in and threatens to sweep me back out to sea. A current seizes me by the heart and begins to pull me back out into the depths. Now, I do not swim alone. There are other footprints next to mine on the shore. Alone, I drown. Together, we survive, recover, and heal.

It is a Process, Not an Event

Recovery, both for substance use disorders and grief, is a process, not an event.

Many books have been written about various models of the stages of grief. Likewise, there have been countless books written about the process of recovery. What the vast majority of them share in common is an understanding that one does not "arrive" or "finish" either recovery or grief. Even so, people do heal, and recovery does happen. We metabolize our grief just as our bodies metabolized our substance. It becomes a part of us, and it changes our ways of seeing the world. Grief can even change our neurochemistry by lowering our serotonin level, leaving us with the sense that things are not "ok" and the feeling that they may never be. In both substance use and grief, healthy choices over time help reawaken the life in us as our brains and bodies heal.

The bad news is that addiction is progressive. The good news is that so is recovery.

As we have more time away from our loss, and as we have more time away from our drug of use, we begin to heal. It is not quick, and it is not easy. It is possible. As we begin to heal, we also begin to recover. To recover is to begin to regain some of the things that we lost while using. That may be a driver's license, money, time, focus, custody of children, relationships, self-worth, or a million other things that are personal to the individual. Recovering these things takes time, and some of them may not be able to be recovered in the same way at all. Time, once gone, is gone. Some relationships cannot be mended. New opportunities may arise, but past opportunities remain in the past. In all of these things, we apply the Serenity Prayer as well. There are some things we can change and some things we cannot, and we seek the wisdom to know the difference.

One other aspect of the recovery process is that the whole family has an opportunity to recover. If you had a member of your immediate family who developed cancer, it would impact everyone in that family. Routines would change. Appointments would arise, and schedules would be disrupted. There would be anxiety and fear. If the person with cancer gets better, the family will have to readjust and will be altered as they learn to move forward together once again. Likewise, the same pattern is true with substance use disorders. We may choose to change our schedules, try to find additional support networks, or endure anxiety and sleepless nights. Even if the loved one gets into recovery, the family is altered. Due to having a loved one in active addiction, family members often lose finances, trust, security, relationships, peace, and sometimes even hope. During my sons' active addiction, nearly everything I said or believed would "never happen to me" did. I spent hundreds of thousands of dollars trying to save my sons from addiction. I lost my marriage. I lost both of my sons. For a time, I lost my way.

These are all reasons that family members can benefit from entering into their own process of recovery. Just like in the case of the substance use disorder, there is no recovery in isolation for the family. Whether it is through Al-Anon, Alateen, Celebrate Recovery, Smart Recovery, the faith community, a civic group, a therapeutic group, a recreational league, or a host of other options, the social support needed for individuals and families to recover are significant and vital. The good news is that these supports do exist.

Once we find our tribe that we can be open, vulnerable, and accepted with, our burdens don't disappear, but they are diminished.

A burden shared is a burden divided.

We are not alone, and we can help to bear one another's loads.

Just Say Yes

In the '80s, for better or for worse, we all knew the mantra related to drug use. "Just Say No" was the order of the day and we were all bombarded with this message in a variety of ways. Was it effective? It's hard to say. One of the challenges with prevention efforts is that it is difficult to demonstrate that something did *not* occur, at least in part, because of one's efforts. Even so, correlations can be and often are made to demonstrate the effectiveness of prevention work. I personally believe that prevention efforts are more difficult today than at any time in history. At least in the '80s the slogan was known and "Just Say No" was a clear and simple message. Today in the general media there is far less clarity.

Individuals, and particularly our youth, are caught in a whirlwind of media campaigns and contradictory information and messages about drugs.

For instance, on the one hand, we tell them marijuana is a drug and can have significant consequences. On the other hand, they hear about a litany of health "benefits" of marijuana use. Our youth may hear of the ravages of the opioid epidemic and yet be prescribed thirty hydrocodone for a simple dental procedure. Alcohol was contained to specific establishments in recent decades. Now, alcohol is ubiquitous in the general public and at community festivals and ball games. Probably the only messaging that has been consistently negative is related to nicotine and tobacco use.

Not surprisingly, use of nicotine has gone down. My point is that messaging matters. "Just Say No" at least had the advantage of being a clear message.

As I look at risk and protective factors related to substance use, if I were designing a prevention program I would probably do almost the opposite of what happened in the '80s. I would call it the "Just Say Yes" campaign. We all have limited time. Every "Yes" that we give is a "No" to something else. Saying "Yes" to healthy friendships will leave less time for unhealthy ones. Saying "Yes" to sports or music groups will leave less time for substance use. These things are not a talisman to ward of any possibility of drug use; Chris's athleticism and Kelly's musical talent are testimonies to that. They are positive social supports that can help protect many from substance use.

The same is true of individuals and families in recovery. I often ask people what their plan is to stay in recovery once they are out of jail or out of treatment. One of the most frightening things I ever hear someone answer is "I'm planning to stay in the house." I usually respond with, "That is wonderful! What are you going to do the second day?" The reality is that no one is going to stay in the house forever, and boredom is a trigger for both substance use and grief. If a person spends even five hours a week using substances and they quit using them, they now have five hours a week that they have to figure out something else to do. Boredom is the enemy, especially in early recovery. I encourage people to find the things they want to say yes to that will help them to schedule and structure their time and then commit to doing them…even on the days when they don't feel like it. Having a person or people who do these things alongside them can be a tremendous help. The general rule that we need other people applies here. We need to do things in community with other people.

Ultimately, simply "not using" is a poor motivator for remaining in recovery. The point of recovery is the things that one wants to recover. In that regard, just saying yes to those things, rediscovering old interests, and discovering new ones can make a significant difference as we learn to restructure our time in recovery.

Control and Influence

One of the biggest challenges for me as I sought to love my sons throughout their struggle with substance use was understanding the difference between control and influence. Before we are parents, and often even when our children are small, many of us suffer from a delusion. The delusion is that we can control them. Some of us feel we can control other human beings as well. One of the hardest lessons for me to learn was that this idea is absurd.

If you have ever had a teething child, then you probably have already encountered this truth. You do everything in your power to help ease their pain and make sure they are ok, but you cannot fix it for them. We sacrifice sleep, use teething rings, and apply medication to ease their suffering, but they still cry. Our best efforts fall short of being able to reach our desired outcome when that outcome is to change another person. Somehow as our children get older and as we love other people in our lives, we forget this lesson. We start thinking that we can somehow change other people through our efforts.

With regard to substance use, we believe that we can somehow out-parent, out-friend, out-demand, out-educate, out-legislate, or even out-counsel the addiction. Just as before, we must consider how well these approaches work for other diseases. Lectures and legislation are impotent in the face of cancer, and they are likewise impotent in the face of addiction. To borrow two words from Jerry Moe at the Betty Ford Center, we did not **cause** the addiction, and we cannot **cure** it either.

This lack of control is not a reason to abdicate the most powerful tool that we do have in our relationships—influence. We cannot control the behavior of another human being, but we can absolutely influence one another. That is an important distinction because for me, at times, it was the difference between insanity and sanity. Earlier I mentioned the Serenity Prayer. For my own mental health, I had to rewrite it for myself some time ago. For me, it now reads as follows:

God grant me the serenity to accept other people,

The courage to change myself,

And the wisdom to know the difference.

I do want to exert all the influence that I possibly can to help a loved one recover. I may encourage, support, talk with, set boundaries with, have interventions with, and do a million other things with an individual to exert that influence. At times, I may even call law enforcement, seek an involuntary commitment, or choose to call social services on a loved one.

These should not be taken lightly and often are best done with some competent support and guidance. Likewise, I might call, talk to, text, or message a loved one to encourage them in their recovery. Each of these are ways to exert influence. Understanding the limitations of our influence is crucial. Ultimately, a person who cares for someone with a substance use disorder can do everything in their power exactly right, and the loved one may not make it.

I have no delusion that I did everything right with Chris or Kelly. I am a fallible human being who loved my boys the best way I knew how. In the end, I lost them both. If love alone could save someone from their addiction, there would be no epidemic. We can't control the disease and those who suffer from it. We will love them the best we know how to provide the best possible opportunity for recovery, but to own another's choices is to own the consequences of those choices. Just as the person struggling with their addiction will grapple with their "powerlessness," so too, must those who love them. If power is control, then we are powerless. If power is influence, then we can use our power to help others find their path to recovery.

Ask Questions

One of the other things that I learned as I sought to find help for my sons was to ask a lot of questions. The world of treatment can be almost as vast of an ocean as the grief was, and the waters can be just as murky at times. Many treatment centers are fine and upstanding institutions, made up of people who are passionate about helping others. Others may be horrific programs that do more harm than benefit. The problem is that horrible programs do not advertise themselves as such. They all do their best to put on a good front.

These programs can look incredibly different. Some may be cinder block buildings with an institutional feel, and others may be palatial buildings on lushly manicured grounds with beautiful coastal or mountain views. Although there is certainly nothing wrong with having nice facilities, the luxuriousness of the program facilities is in no way predictive of treatment outcomes.

The length of stay and staff qualifications can likewise run the gamut. Programs may be a short-term hospital stay of a few days. They may be a twenty-eight-day residential program or a long-term treatment facility.

Services could include a "halfway house," a "three-quarters house," or a recovery house or community. It may be a college recovery community. It may be an outpatient program. They may have licensed staff or staff of only people in recovery. Lengths of service and credentials of staff vary significantly between programs.

The clinical approach may also vary. A program may focus on the Twelve Steps. It may focus on evidence-based practices. It may offer family supports or treatment. It may encourage involvement in mutual support groups. It may have, or it may refuse to have medically appropriate treatment. It may or may not consider co-mingling diagnoses and treatment. It may or may not utilize drug testing as a part of their evaluation and treatment.

The key here is that few people take the time to ask questions about the program or services a loved one might be receiving. If you do not ask these questions, many less scrupulous programs are not likely to offer the answers to them, particularly if the answer casts them in a less than favorable light. Most of us would not dream of buying a car without reading a bit about the vehicle, looking at the sticker in the window, and taking it for a test drive. Many programs cost significantly more than a vehicle and the stakes are significantly higher for our loved ones. Even so, many of us would bring a loved one to a program and drop them off without reading their reviews online and paying attention to who posted the reviews. Some of us would not think to ask to see the actual room our loved one would be staying in or the place where they eat. Asking such things is a means of once again using the influence that we do have to attempt to guide our loved one to the best possible treatment that we can find.

Just as with the advertisements for programs and facilities, reported success rates vary wildly. The first step is asking what success means. If they can't define it, that's a pretty good indicator that is not where you want your loved one to be. Asking questions about follow-up and aftercare can be a tremendous help in planning for the loved one's return to the community.

Asking about what happens if a loved one's insurance runs out, if applicable, can likewise help ensure that they don't find themselves put out of a program in the middle of the night somewhere during a time when they are most vulnerable.

There are resources online about what treatment is and questions to ask about programs and facilities as well. A few minutes of reading and a few minutes of assertiveness in asking questions has the potential to help avoid a lifetime of heartache. Don't hesitate to ask lots of questions and be cautious of those who hesitate to answer them.

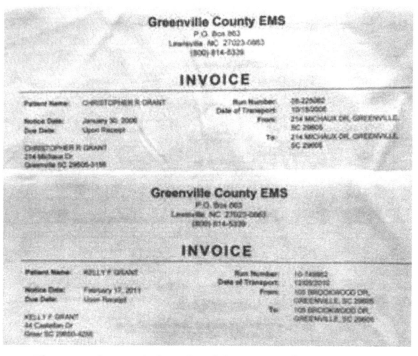

There are often reminders of one's loss. Some of these may span throughout the calendar year and can extend for years. The first holidays without a loved one can be particularly difficult. Some days such as birthdays, death days, and other special events can be especially painful. Other reminders come much more quickly. Following the death of a loved one, emergency medical services usually transport the body of the deceased. Shortly following the death of both Chris and Kelly, I received bills from EMS for the ambulance ride of my sons. Although some days are harder than others, the general movement is towards healing over time. The pain does eventually consume you less, and life does eventually grow out beyond the edges of it.

There is Honor in Grief

In these pages, I have sought to be transparent and vulnerable. I did not do a perfect job of being a spouse, a father, or a loved one to those who struggle with substance use disorders. I still don't. The grief is there, but the difference is that now there is purpose in it. I know what it is to suffer the loss of a loved one, and I have every intention of doing everything in my power and influence to help another human being not have to endure that loss. I also intend to use any influence I have to let others, who are struggling, directly or indirectly with substance use disorders, know that they are not alone. Finally, I will use my influence to let those who have lost someone know that they, too, are not alone.

I do not know exactly how you feel, but I know what it is to lose someone you love and to be lost in the ocean of grief for a time. I also know that, eventually, you too, can find your way to shore. In the meantime, I and many others, stand ready to swim beside you. Together, we can recover.

One of the truths that it has taken me a long time to see is that there is tremendous honor in grief. One thing that is seldom acknowledged or understood is that we grieve most what we have loved most. To grieve Chris and Kelly is to grieve the loss of the incredible human beings they were, the lives they touched, and the relationships that we shared. The degree of the grief is related to the degree of the love. When we lose someone distant from us, the pain is remote. When we lose someone close, the pain is visceral and can seem insurmountable.

When someone we love dies, part of what we miss is all the things we count on them to know—the inside jokes, the names of the places and people you can't recall, old recipes and phone numbers, the names of songs and movies, traditions, and stories. We miss the ability to revisit those memories and fact check them against one another. We miss the parts of the relationship that no one else would understand. In short, we miss the "us" that we shared and the parts of it we can't experience without them. When someone we love dies, they always take a part of us with them, and we always keep a piece of them close to our hearts as well. This is the honor that is intrinsic in the grief that we experience. We only grieve that which we love.

I grieve Chris and Kelly so deeply precisely because I love them so deeply. For me, part of my legacy consists of honoring their lives through how I live my own now, of ensuring that I do not waste one ounce of the pain we've endured. Our heartache becomes the broken spaces where we best connect, empathize with, and can encourage others that things can get better.

There is Hope

I have set out to share this story of my family and my personal grief for one primary purpose–to share hope. Even in the face of the loss of my two sons, I have tremendous hope today. I have immense hope even in the face of the opioid epidemic that, according to the Center for Disease Control, claimed more than 72,000 lives in 2017. I have this hope because I have experienced it firsthand.

My hope is not the untested, hand-me-down, trite-phrased messages of greeting cards and awkward condolences. My hope was forged in the fire of loss and with what remained after the fire went out. My hope came when I survived the deep waters and discovered that there is still a shore. I walk on the shore and feel the solidity of the sand beneath my feet again. Most of all, I have hope that I can be of help to others who are still at sea to find their way back to solid ground again.

I have seen firsthand people struggling with addiction find a vibrant and sustainable recovery.

I have seen families where addiction has been a destructive force, begin to mend and learn to love and trust one another again. I have seen people rediscover, and in some cases, discover for the first time, who they are and what sets their spirit on fire with passion.

I have seen recovery.

Regardless of how I may feel on a given day, I can choose to cling to what I know.

And what do I know?

Today I know that:

If you feel that you cannot make it, you can.

If you feel that you cannot recover, you can.

If you feel that that you cannot go on, you can.

If you feel there is nothing left to live for, there is.

If you feel the pain will never end, it will.

If you feel you can make it on your own, you're wrong.

If you feel you cannot make it alone, you're right.

If you feel you are all alone, I'm here with countless others.

If you think that this will be easy, it won't.

These truths do not negate your feelings. That is a lie that has led many to despair and to the point of giving up. The simple truth (not easy, but simple) is that sometimes in the face of how we feel, we have to cling to what we know.

Life can get better.

You can learn to laugh again.

You can begin to heal.

You can find gratitude even in the midst of grief.

You can recover.

You are not alone.

There. Is. Hope.

Let's love ourselves well enough to be real, authentic, and vulnerable.

Let's love each other well enough to encourage one another to do the same.

Let's lovingly accept one another as we are.

Let's love others well enough to help them towards the shore.

The waters of grief may be deep, but the shores of recovery are wider.

May we reach them together.

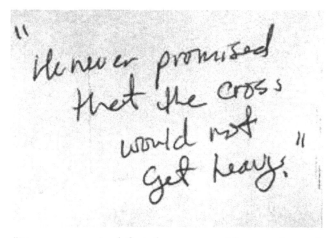

"He never promised that the cross would not get heavy."
This is a note that I wrote during a church service following
the loss of both sons.

CONCLUSION

The Good That Follows

I would not have chosen the path that I have walked, but I have seen some of the good things that have grown up through the cracks that losing Chris and Kelly left behind.

For starters, the death of both of my sons had a tremendous impact on the lives of their friends. I have stayed in touch with many of them in the years since Chris and Kelly's deaths, and I consulted with several of them in writing this story. They have helped me to fill in some of the details that I did not know firsthand. In staying in touch with them, I have seen a number of both Chris's and Kelly's friends quit using drugs since the death of my sons. I even learned that the young man who introduced Kelly to heroin has not used at all since Kelly died.

Kelly was awarded his Psychology degree from the College of Charleston posthumously. Upon review of his transcripts in 2016, the college informed us that he had enough credits to graduate.

The founding of Chris and Kelly's HOPE Foundation has been a significant part of my moving from grief to gratitude and transforming some of my heartaches into helping those who struggle with addiction. The Foundation is a 501c3 organization that operates under the auspices of the Community Foundation of Greenville. It was created in honor of Chris and Kelly Grant to financially assist organizations and programs whose purpose is to help adolescents and young adults who are struggling with substance abuse, addiction, and depression.

The objective of the foundation is to financially assist and support agencies and programs who are many times too small and "under the radar" to receive funds from much larger foundations but who nevertheless do great work at the true grassroots level and save lives through their efforts.

We seek to assist those groups in all their aspects of the addiction spectrum, including:

- Early education in schools
- Community organizations that promote healthy development
- Prevention
- Intervention
- Treatment
- Aftercare/Housing
- The science of addiction
- Collegiate recovery programs
- Financial support to assist larger organizations and foundations who have the ability to reach thousands of people

Through the Chris and Kelly's HOPE Foundation, we have the opportunity to help support many agencies in their work of helping others recover from substance use disorders. We believe in this work, which is why a portion of the proceeds from this book are being reinvested back into Chris and Kelly's HOPE to continue making a difference in the lives of those suffering with substance use disorders and those who love them.

One of the most meaningful contributions that Chris and Kelly's HOPE Foundation made was to build a fitness park at a local residential treatment facility for adolescent males. This was personally meaningful to me because it was the sort of thing that I know Chris and Kelly would have both enjoyed using during their teens. It encourages health both for the young men in the facility as well as the community. Trey Gowdy, former United States Representative from South Carolina's 4th District, spoke at the dedication for the park and many local officials attended as well. This was evidence to me that many in public office do have a heart for those struggling with addiction. We can be a part of both raising awareness of the problem of addiction, and we can be a part of the solution in helping people on their path to recovery.

Good and healing can eventually come from even incredibly difficult, heart-wrenching circumstances.

Nothing can ever replace my two sons, but my sincere hope is to spare other families the sorrow of a similar loss and to walk alongside those who may already be in the midst of a similar heartache.

Chris and Kelly's HOPE Foundation has had the opportunity to support numerous other agencies and organizations since its formation. Although not a complete list, some of these include:

Aerosmith Program, SC

Archway Institute, FL

Any Length Recovery (15 scholarships), Sumter, SC

Atlanta Harm Reduction Coalition, GA

Ben Lucas Foundation, Greenville, SC

Boy Scouts of America, Greenville, SC

Brandi's Wish, FL

Campus Recovery Clemson and Sober, SC

Canterbury Counseling, Greenville, SC

Center for Drug and Alcohol Programs at MUSC, Charleston, SC
Change Attitudes Now (CAN), Spartanburg, SC
Child Evangelism Fellowship, Greenville, SC
Children's Aid and Family Service, Paramus, NJ
Christ Church Episcopal School Red Ribbon Week, Greenville, SC
Clean Break, FL, NC, SC, and TN
Coaches for Character, Greenville, SC
College of Charleston Campus Recovery, Charleston, SC
Connie Maxwell Children's Home, Greenwood, SC
Cooper Riis, NC
Creighton's House, Charleston, SC
Creighton Shipman's 22 Forever Foundation, Charleston, SC
Crossbridge Family Ministries, Summerville, SC
Dr. James Dobson Family Talk, CO
Facing Addictions, CT
Faces and Voices of Recovery (FAVOR), Charleston, SC
Faces and Voices of Recovery (FAVOR), Greenville, SC
Faces and Voices of Recovery (FAVOR), Spartanburg, SC
Faith Home, Greenwood, SC
Families for Sensible Drug Policy, PA
Fellowship of Christian Athletes, Greenville, SC
First Contact Drug Addiction Ministry, NC
First Impressions, Greenville, SC
Fisher DeBerry Foundation, CO
Gateway House, Greenville, SC
Generations Group Home, Greenville, SC
Greenville Children's Hospital, Greenville, SC
Greenville High School Booster Club, Greenville, SC
Greer Community Ministries, Greer, SC
Greer Relief and Resources Agency, Greer, SC
Hale House Foundation, GA

Harris House Foundation, MO

Haven of Rest Ministries, OH

Hire Heroes USA, GA

Homes of Hope, Greenville, SC

HopeRx, NC

John Knox Presbyterian Church, Greenville, SC

Junior Achievement, Greenville, SC

Just Say Something, Greenville, SC

Langston Charter School, Simpsonville, SC

Michael's Voice, Charlotte, NC

Miracle Hill Ministries Overcomer's Program, Greenville, SC

Montford Hall, Asheville, NC

Ohio State Recovery Campus, OH

Operation Santa Claus, Greenville, SC

Our Lady of the Rosary Red Ribbon Week

Paramus High School, NJ

Pavillon, NC

Pavillon Place, Greenville, SC

Pickens County Behavioral Health Services, Pickens, SC

Penn State Recovery Campus, PA

Rutgers University Recovery Campus, NJ

Salvation Army Men's Recovery Program, Greenville, SC

Sam Wells Addiction Interventions, Charleston, SC

Serenity Place, Greenville, SC

Sober Living for Jesus, TN

South Carolina Charities, SC

St. Anthony's Red Ribbon Week, Greenville, SC

St. Joseph's Red Ribbon Week, Greenville, SC

St. Mary's Red Ribbon Week, Greenville, SC

St. Teresa Catholic Church, Summerville, SC

Stepping Up Coalition, Atlanta, GA

Turning Point, Greenville, SC
The Community Foundation of Middle Tennessee, TN
The Family Effect, Greenville, SC
The Phoenix Center, Greenville, SC
Three-Dimensional Life, GA
UNLV-Reno Recovery Campus, NV
Upstate Fatherhood Coalition, Greenville, SC
Victoria's Voice, FL
Wake Up Carolina, Charleston, SC
Western Carolina University Recovery Campus, NC
White Horse Academy, Greenville, SC

To join us in our mission of helping others find their path to healing through recovery, please reach out to us, request a speaker, or contribute through the following:

To request a speaking engagement with Steve Grant or to donate to the Chris and Kelly's HOPE Foundation, please visit the ChrisKellyHOPE website or send your donation to the address below.

Chris and Kelly's HOPE Foundation
c/o The Community Foundation of Greenville
630 E. Washington Street, Suite A
Greenville, SC 29601

To request a speaking engagement with James:
James Campbell, LPC, LAC, MAC, CACII
864-360-1636

For questions about donations:
Bob Morris - 864.233.5925 tel

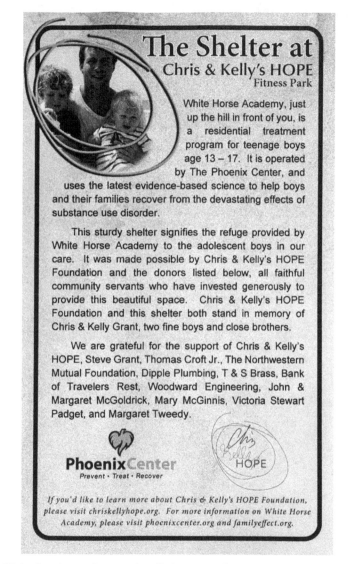

The Shelter at
Chris & Kelly's HOPE
Fitness Park

White Horse Academy, just up the hill in front of you, is a residential treatment program for teenage boys age 13 – 17. It is operated by The Phoenix Center, and uses the latest evidence-based science to help boys and their families recover from the devastating effects of substance use disorder.

This sturdy shelter signifies the refuge provided by White Horse Academy to the adolescent boys in our care. It was made possible by Chris & Kelly's HOPE Foundation and the donors listed below, all faithful community servants who have invested generously to provide this beautiful space. Chris & Kelly's HOPE Foundation and this shelter both stand in memory of Chris & Kelly Grant, two fine boys and close brothers.

We are grateful for the support of Chris & Kelly's HOPE, Steve Grant, Thomas Croft Jr., The Northwestern Mutual Foundation, Dipple Plumbing, T & S Brass, Bank of Travelers Rest, Woodward Engineering, John & Margaret McGoldrick, Mary McGinnis, Victoria Stewart Padget, and Margaret Tweedy.

PhoenixCenter
Prevent · Treat · Recover

HOPE

If you'd like to learn more about Chris & Kelly's HOPE Foundation, please visit chriskellyhope.org. For more information on White Horse Academy, please visit phoenixcenter.org and familyeffect.org.

This sign is at Chris and Kelly's HOPE fitness park located at a residential treatment facility for adolescent males in Greenville, SC. The park was donated to help provide the teens served in the program support for becoming even healthier in their recovery.

Gratitude and Testimonials

received
7/31/17

Dear Etta,

First off I want to thank you from the bottom of my heart. This opportunity you have given me has been great and you saved my life. I was in a very dark place when I first spoke with you. I am taking it day by day and its getting better. You were there for me when no one else was and words cant describe what that means to me. This place is great. All the residents here seem to want and some have what I want. I thank you in my prayers on a daily basis. Now hopfully my daughter will know what its like to have a sober father. I go to work now everyday. I pay my rent and I even now grocery shop and do laundry. LOL! Its an amazing feeling to finally start being an adult. People like you are very rare and I promise to hold my end of our deal. Soon I will be able to use the phone here and I will call so we can chat some. Your an amazing person and GOD has a special place in heaven for you. Please feel free to write me anything you want to. Again I thank you so much. Your a life saver and an angel in my eyes. I hope more people like me find someone like you. THANKS soooooo MUCH and I will make you proud of me.

Your Friend,

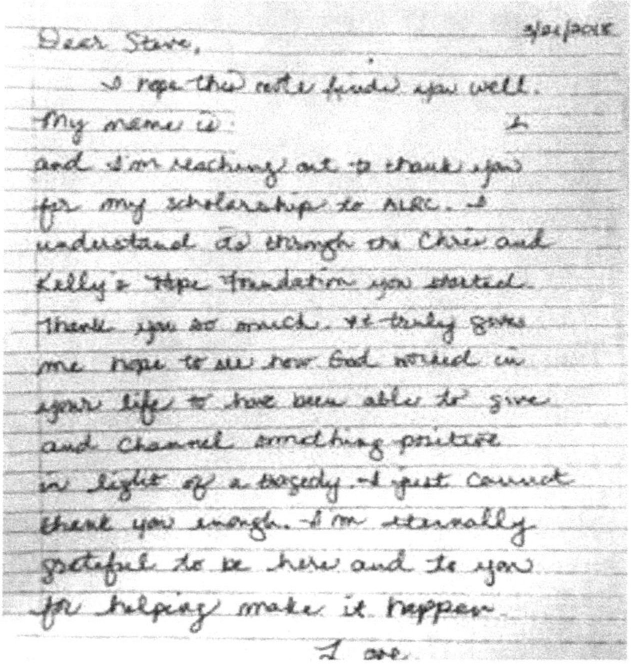

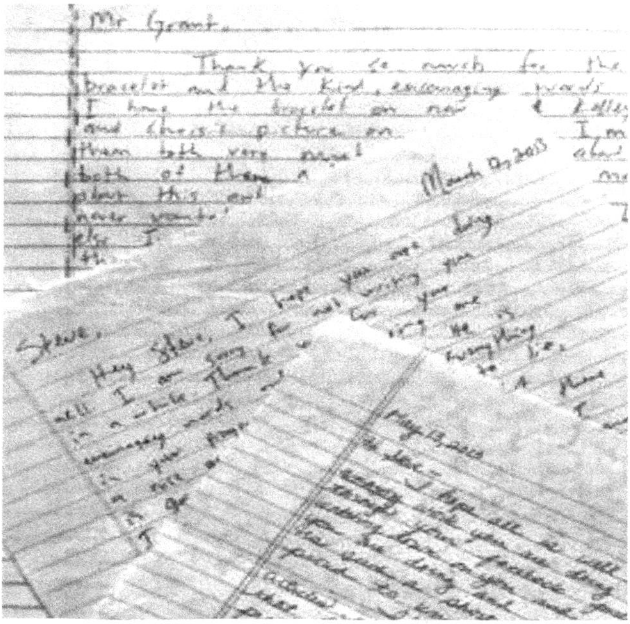

This is a photo of Chris's hand reaching towards the sky. It serves as a consistent reminder to me to reach beyond where I am in this moment and to cast my eyes to the horizon. There is comfort. There is healing, and there is tremendous, tremendous hope.

ABOUT THE AUTHORS

Steve Grant

Steve Grant has been in the financial services business since 1982. He was born in New York City and raised in Paramus, New Jersey. He founded the Chris and Kelly's HOPE Foundation in March of 2012 and serves as its Executive Director. Steve is the four-time recipient of Northwestern Mutual's Foundation Community Service Award. In 2013, he was presented with the South Carolina Upstate Philanthropic Achievement Award. In 2015, Steve received the South Carolina Governor's Volunteer Award for volunteer community leadership.

Steve is a graduate of Furman University. He currently serves on both The Family Effect Board as well as the Board of The Center for Drug and Alcohol Programs/Medical University of SC.

Steve resides in Simpsonville, SC with his wife, Cathy.

James E. Campbell, LPC, LAC, MAC, CACII

James Campbell has been working professionally in the human services field for over twenty-three years. His passion is helping people, families, and relationships to heal and assisting them in building on the strengths they possess.

James is a Licensed Professional Counselor, a Licensed Addiction Counselor, a Master Addictions Counselor, a Certified Addictions Counselor II through SCAADAC, and is a member of both NAADAC and ACA. James currently serves as the president of SCAADAC.

James is the Founder of Family Excellence, Inc., the Director and Lead Trainer of Family Excellence Institute, LLC, and is a nationally recognized author and sought-after speaker.

James resides in South Carolina with his wonderful wife (Amy), daughter (Erin), son (Jonathan), and their ornery dog (Marshall).

ACKNOWLEDGMENTS AND GRATITUDE

From Steve

I would like to extend my sincere thanks to my Lord and Savior Jesus Christ, my wife Cathy, to mine and Cathy's families who have stayed by me during good and bad times, to all my friends (especially John and Susan Lady for all their support and my long-time friend David Ellison), Ben Newman and John O'Leary for the inspiration to start Chris and Kelly's HOPE, Bob Morris and his staff at The Community Foundation of Greenville for all their help getting Chris and Kelly's HOPE Foundation off the ground and for their ongoing support, Stacey Bevill who maintains our website and provides other marketing services, Mary-Lu Bonte and my other long-term associates at Northwestern Mutual, Scott Dishman, Steve Pulley, The Family Effect, Bill Reynolds, Anna Carr, The Center for Drug and Alcohol Programs at the Medical University of South Carolina, and "Just Say Something." I would also like to thank Terry Whalin with Morgan James Publishing, Dennis and Susie Welch with Articulate, and Mark and Donna Johnston with the Greenville Journal. To Lori and Larry Stuart, thank you for the inspiration to complete this book.

From James

I would like to express my gratitude to my Lord and Savior, Jesus Christ, who has walked with me in my grief and carried me when I stumbled. I am also incredibly grateful to Amy, Erin, Jonathan, and all of my family for their ongoing love and support. I am especially grateful to my sister, Wendy, one of the bravest people I have ever known. I am thankful for the many individuals and families who have trusted me enough to walk with them in their grief and for friends who have loved me enough to walk with me through my own.

In particular, I am both grateful for and inspired by the courage and transparency of Steve Grant in sharing his story of both loss and of healing with me and with all who read these pages.

I am grateful for mentors and friends who have taught me a great deal about life, love, loss, addiction, recovery, grief, and healing; specifically, I would like to thank Jeff Georgi, Alan Lyme, Cardwell C. Nuckols, and Trude Scharff for their guidance, friendship, compassion, and wisdom.

Lastly, I am thankful to every individual and organization who helps guide, support, encourage, and walk alongside those who have either not yet found or who are already on their path to recovery.

WEED AND THE ADOLESCENT BRAIN

For some, weed is a gateway drug. It certainly was for my son, Chris. It is not my intention to state my opinions about marijuana; I simply want to share some of the research about cannabis and the impact it has on the adolescent brain. I was fortunate to hear Allan L. Barger, MSW, speak and he introduced me to the information I wish to share with you.

In July 2017, the American Journal of Public Health published "Lower-Risk Cannabis Use Guidelines: A Comprehensive Update of Evidence and Recommendations.[1]" According to this article, 25-30% of adolescents or young adults reported using cannabis within the past year. The paper was written to address the common use of cannabis in North America, especially among young people. Since some cannabis-related health outcomes may be influenced by behaviors that can be changed the goal is to provide a valuable prevention tool to improve public health outcomes.

The following information is included in the article referenced above:

---

1   American Journal of Public Health, *Lower-Risk Cannabis Use Guidelines: A Comprehensive Update of Evidence and Recommendations*, by Benedikt Fischer PhD, Cayley Russell MA, Pamela Sabioni PhD, Wim van den Brink MD, PhD, Bernard Le Foll MD, PhD, Wayne Hall PhD, Jürgen Rehm PhD, and Robin Room PhD, Published July 12, 2017

"There is substantial evidence that early onset (e.g., before age 18 years) cannabis use is associated with a higher risk of dependence and later problem outcomes. This may be because cannabis use in adolescence impairs various aspects of brain development, especially if intensive and ongoing during the brain development period (until the mid-20s). For example, early-onset cannabis users have shown alterations of white and gray brain matter and cortical thickness; lowered functional connectivity, IQ, and cognitive functioning; and greater behavioral impulsivity. These may reflect factors explaining both early onset of cannabis use and later outcomes."

Associations between early-onset cannabis use and mental health problems and dependence outcomes are well-established. Compared with later onset, early-onset users commonly used cannabis more intensively and subsequently showed poorer cognitive and executive functioning. The risk of cannabis dependence was almost double in early- versus late-onset users (1 in 6 vs 1 in 10, respectively). Among cannabis-dependent users, early onset is associated with subsequent poorer attention, verbal learning and memory, impulse control, and executive functioning outcomes.

Individual studies have documented further associations for early-onset use, for example with elevated risk of developing mental health problems, including depressive symptoms, and psychotic symptoms. Conversely, no associations were found between cannabis use and psychosis, or reduced IQ, among those initiating use after age 18 years."

RESOURCES

The phone numbers below are for national hotlines that can help direct you to resources in your area and are current as of this printing.

Al-Anon
1-757-563-1600
Alcoholics Anonymous (AA)
1-212-870-3400
Facing Addiction with NCADD
1-800-622-2255
National Alliance on Mental Illness (NAMI)
1-800-950-6264
Narcotics Anonymous (NA)
1-818-773-9999 ext.771
National Institute on Drug Abuse (NIDA)
1-301-443-1124
Substance Abuse and Mental Health Services Alliance (SAMHSA)
1-877-726-4727
Faces and Voices of Recovery (FAVOR)
1-202-737-0690

CPSIA information can be obtained
at www.ICGtesting.com
Printed in the USA
LVHW110923081120
671036LV00005B/188

9 781642 795486